Prepared by the CRMS project team with generous support from the Institute of Museum and Library Services.

This project was made possible in part by the Institute of Museum and Library Services (Grant Number LG-05-14-0042-14). The views, findings, conclusions, or recommendations expressed in this publication do not necessarily represent those of the Institute of Museum and Library Services.

THE COPYRIGHT REVIEW MANAGEMENT SYSTEM

http://www.lib.umich.edu/imls-national-leadership-grant-crms-world

What It Is

Working over a span of nearly eight years, the University of Michigan Library received three grants from the Institute of Museum and Library Services (IMLS) to generously fund CRMS, a cooperative effort by partner research libraries to identify books in the public domain in HathiTrust.

In **CRMS-US (2008–11)**, CRMS reviewed over 170,000 volumes in the HathiTrust Digital Library that were published in the United States between 1923 and 1963 ("CRMS-US"). That first project team—which included reviewers from the University of Michigan, the University of Wisconsin, the University of Minnesota, and Indiana University—identified nearly 87,000 volumes as being in the public domain, in addition to collecting renewal information and identifying rights holders of works in copyright.

In **CRMS-World (2011–14)**, we built on that accomplishment by reviewing an additional 110,000 US volumes and expanded the scope of the review to include 170,000 English-language volumes published in Canada, the United Kingdom, and Australia between 1872 and 1944 ("CRMS-World"). This second grant continued through the end of 2014 and included initial development on an interface for works from Spain, a process for quality control, and an expanded suite of materials to allow an expert member of our project team to train and monitor reviewers online.

The current **CRMS grant (2014–16)** simultaneously made possible continued copyright review of CRMS-World volumes, the development of this toolkit, and planning related to the long-term sustainability of CRMS. We are hopeful that, whatever the near term brings for CRMS as an individual project, the valuable work of identifying public domain works will continue. We are grateful for the support and collaboration of all who have touched this project.

FINDING THE PUBLIC DOMAIN

Copyright Review Management System Toolkit

IMLS National Leadership Grant
Project Grant: Advancing Digital Resources

© *Regents of the University of Michigan*, CC BY 4.0
Richard C. Adler
Justin Bonfiglio
Kristina Eden
Brian S. Hall
Melissa Levine
University of Michigan Library Copyright Office

You are free to:

Share: copy and redistribute the material in any medium or format

Adapt: remix, transform, and build upon the material for any purpose, even commercially

The licensor cannot revoke these freedoms as long as you follow the terms of the license.

Under the following terms:

Attribution: You must give appropriate credit, provide a link to the license, and indicate if changes were made. You may do so in any reasonable manner, but not in any way that suggests the licensor endorses you or your use.

No additional restrictions: you may not apply legal terms or technological measures that legally restrict others from doing anything the license permits.

https://creativecommons.org/licenses/by/4.0

Recommended Attribution: *Finding the Public Domain: Copyright Review Management System Toolkit*, © 2016, Regents of the University of Michigan, is licensed under CC-BY 4.0

Manufactured in the United States of America

ISBN 978-1-60785-373-2
ISBN 978-1-60785-374-9 (e-book)

Contents

Copyright as a Design Problem — xv

Acknowledgments — xix

About the Copyright Review Management System Toolkit — 1

Getting Started — 3
- How to Use This Toolkit — 3
- Preplanning Document 1: Building Your Team — 5
    - 1. Project Manager — 5
    - 2. Legal Expert — 6
    - 3. Developer — 8
    - 4. Training and Reviewer Manager (Quality Control) — 9
    - 5. Copyright Reviewers — 10
- Preplanning Document 2: Building Your Project — 12
    - Institutional Commitment — 12
    - Project Design — 12
    - Data Collection — 14
    - Legal — 15
    - Project Management — 16
    - Training — 17
    - Process — 17
    - Technical Considerations — 18
    - Verification — 19
    - Funding — 19

CONTENTS

Preplanning Document 3: CRMS Project Decision Points	20
Foreign Language/Script	21
Inserts	21
Translations	21
Dissertation/Thesis	21
Periodicals	22
Non–Class A Works (United States)	22
Editions	22
Government Works	23
Author-Based Determinations	23

At a Glance—Overview 25

Leadership	25
Project Scoping	26
Legal	29
Personnel	30
Copyright Review	32
Documentation	34
Output/Access Decisions	35
Verification	35
Funding	36

Involving Your Leadership 39

Dean and Library Administrators	39
Office of General Counsel	40
HathiTrust Leadership	41
Advisory Working Group	42

CONTENTS

Project Scoping — 43
- The Scope of CRMS-US — 43
- The Scope of CRMS-World — 46
- An Alternate Approach: Author-Based Scoping — 48
- Another Approach for US Works:
  - Copyright Notice–Based Review — 50
- Application: US State Government Documents — 51

Legal — 53
- About This Legal Section — 53
- CRMS-US: Building Copyright Expertise — 54
- Duration of Copyright in the US — 56
  - Application: US State Government Documents (1923–77) — 60
  - 17 U.S.C. § 104A: Copyright Restoration under the URAA — 61
  - US Federal Government Documents (17 U.S.C. § 105) — 64
- CRMS-World: Building International Copyright Expertise — 66
  - Territoriality — 67
  - National Treatment — 68
  - Special Cases — 69
  - King James Bible — 70
  - Peter Pan — 71
  - Crown Copyright — 73
- Additional Considerations — 74
  - Inserts — 75
  - Published versus Unpublished — 78
  - Application: Dissertations and Theses — 80
  - Additional Authors — 83

CONTENTS

Translations	84
Multipart Monographs	85
Observations	**86**
The Importance of the und/nfi Category	86
Notice and Takedown	89
Role of an Advisory Working Group: Oversight from Copyright Experts	90
Partnership and Collaborative Work	91

Personnel   95

Selecting Reviewers	95
Time Commitments	97
Security and Authorizing Reviewers for Access	99
Training	101
Distance Learning	103
Sandbox	104
Other Training Tools	105
Readiness for Production	107
Reviewer Communication	108
Benchmarking and Ongoing Reviewer Management	110
Experts	111
Supervisor Communication	112
Cost-Share Reports	113

CONTENTS

Verification — 115
  Double Review — 115
  Copyright Review Verification — 116
    Preproject Verification — 116
    Stage 1: Process Verification — 117
    Stage 2: Results Verification — 119

Funding — 121
  Cost-Share Reporting — 121
  Challenges to Flexibility — 122
  Institutional Funding — 124

Technical — 125
  About This Technical Section — 125
    Background — 125
  A Glossary of Terms Useful for Copyright Determination — 128
    1. Objects Being Reviewed ("Candidate Pool") — 128
    2. User Roles — 134
    3. Interface and System — 136
    4. Rights Determination — 138
  Technical Components — 141
  Core Elements — 142
    Web-Based Application Infrastructure — 142
    CRMS Database — 143
    Algorithms/Heuristics for Identifying Which Works Are In-Scope — 145
    A Queuing Algorithm That Presents the Right Volumes to the Right People — 147

CONTENTS

Review Interface with Information Resources Appropriate
    to the Research   148
A Way to Export Determinations   152

Critical Advanced Elements   **153**

Appropriate Access Controls   153
An Algorithm to Provide Recommended Judgments   156
A Mechanism for Resolving Conflicting Reviews   157

Recommended Elements   **158**

A Way to Link a Given Determination with a Set of Reviews   159
A Means for Reviewers to Put Their Review Temporarily
    "On Hold"   159
Inheriting Rights Determinations on Otherwise
    Identical Volumes   160
A "Subproject" Mechanism That Allows Assignment of Volumes
    and Reviewers to Specific Sets of Works for Review   161
A Mechanism to Detect When Re-review Is Likely to
    Be Profitable   163
Tools for Searching Various Categories of Reviews   163
Reviewer Performance Statistics Pages   165
Priority   167
A Mechanism for Overseeing New Reviewer Performance   167

The CRMS Review Processes   **168**

Zephir and the HathiTrust Rights Database   169
Criteria for Identifying In-Scope Volumes   170
The Candidates Pool   172
The Queue   174
The HathiTrust PageTurner Access and Authentication Modules   177

CONTENTS

The Review Process	180
System Response to Matches and Conflicts	181
Expert Adjudication	184
Overnight Processing	186
Inheritance	187
CRMS Exports and the HathiTrust Rights Database	190
Pilot Projects	**193**
Reviewing Works Published in Spain	**193**
Introduction	194
Project Design	195
Workflow	196
Final Observations	199
Outcomes	200
Latin American Works from the Benson Collection at University of Texas at Austin	**201**
Introduction	202
Project Design	203
Workflow	205
Final Observations	206
Outcomes	207
Humboldt University of Berlin: Rights Research Project for German Books	**208**
Introduction	209
Project Design	210
Workflow	211

CONTENTS

Final Observations	212
Outcomes	213
Contributing to Name Authority Cooperative Program (NACO) Records	**214**
Introduction	215
Project Design	216
Workflow	217
Final Observations	219
Outcomes	220
US State Government Documents	**221**
Introduction	221
Project Design	222
Workflow	224
Final Observations	226
Outcomes	227
Appendices	**229**
Rights and Reason Codes	234
Excerpts from the CRMS-World Wiki	236
Single Authorship	238
Author Death Date Not Found	238
Approximate Death Dates	239
Author Name Missing from Title Page	239
Late Author	239
Foreign Language Works with English Front Matter	239
Compilations and Anthologies	240
Sheet Music or Musical Compositions	241

CONTENTS

CRMS-World Training Test 1   241
CRMS-World Training Test 2   251

Glossary   283

Resources   291

Index   295

- GETTING STARTED
- AT A GLANCE – OVERVIEW
- INVOLVING YOUR LEADERSHIP
- PROJECT SCOPING
- LEGAL
- PERSONNEL
- VERIFICATION
- FUNDING
- TECHNICAL
- PILOT PROJECTS

Preface

> Nothing happens unless first a dream.
>
> —Carl Sandburg

COPYRIGHT AS A DESIGN PROBLEM

Copyright is meant to *do* something—several things—to accomplish socially desirable ends. One of those ends is to create a space for a free exchange of ideas that allows us to build upon a universe of expression that came before. The world is a rich place because of authors, and it is enriched further by works of authorship in the public domain that anyone can copy, rearrange, and repurpose in any way they choose. This toolkit is an example of the tremendous work that can be accomplished when we are free to build on what has come before.

How can I tell if something is in the public domain? This is the central question addressed daily by the Copyright Review Management System (CRMS) project. It is a special question and one essential to the social bargain that society has struck with authors and rights holders.

It is also a deceptively simple question. There *should* be a straightforward answer, especially for books. It *should* be easy to know when something is—or is not—subject to copyright. At first glance, books look like straightforward artifacts. And yet, in an age of absolute fluidity of media and medium, even plain old books can be highly complex embodiments of copyright. We need to make it easier to ascertain whether a work is in the public domain. Indeed, recognition and respect for the public domain is a fundamental part of the social bargain of copyright. The interests of "rights holders" and "users" are often framed as in antithesis to one another. In the bigger picture, the two are intertwined. If the rights of copyright holders are to be respected and valued as part of

PREFACE

the social bargain, the public domain as a matter of copyright law should be ascertainable and enjoyed.

Given this complexity, consider the determination of the copyright status of a given creative work as a design problem. How do we move the copyright status of works in the collections of our libraries, museums, and archives from confusion and uncertainty to clarity and opportunity? The earliest planners of CRMS—including John Wilkin, Anne Karle-Zenith, and Judith Ahronheim—recognized that if we are to shine light on the public domain, we must design systems to help us move from an opaque copyright landscape to one more clearly defined. Their determined efforts and the creation of the HathiTrust Digital Library made CRMS possible. For over six years, we have been building on their foundational work, iteratively refining our approach to the design problem of copyright research. We have a great deal to share from our experience.

The first thing we want to share is a sense of possibility. We have always recognized that copyright law and the application of that law are complex and only grow more so in a global framework. At the same time, we have come to appreciate that reasonable, committed, hardworking information professionals with the help of good counsel can navigate that complexity to great effect. CRMS has taught us that we can illuminate the public domain on a large scale, with hundreds of thousands of public domain works identified to date. This is no small feat, and we hope it will inspire others as they pursue similarly ambitious projects.

PREFACE

We also want to share our appreciation. CRMS was a significant effort involving well over sixty professionals spread across nineteen partner institutions. It drew on the experience and good guidance of countless colleagues. It also used tools like the Stanford Copyright Renewal Database, the Virtual International Authority File (VIAF), and a host of other efforts to identify and describe authors all around the world. CRMS would not have been possible without the visionary decisions that built and continue to build HathiTrust. The tools others have built, combined with expertise provided by our colleagues and the collaborative spirit of our partners, humble us and enrich the work we do. We are sincerely grateful for the efforts of our community.

> Melissa Levine
> Lead Copyright Officer,
> University of Michigan Library
> Ann Arbor, Michigan
> May 16, 2016

- GETTING STARTED
- AT A GLANCE—OVERVIEW
- INVOLVING YOUR LEADERSHIP
- PROJECT SCOPING
- LEGAL
- PERSONNEL
- VERIFICATION
- FUNDING
- TECHNICAL
- PILOT PROJECTS

Acknowledgments

This toolkit represents the work of the CRMS team at the University of Michigan, with funding and support from the Institute for Museum and Library Services in the form of three National Leadership Grants (LG-05-08-0141-08, LG-05-11-0150-11, and LG-05-14-0042-14). We are cognizant of the unique place of the National Leadership Grants and the IMLS's significant role in stewarding these precious resources for the benefit of the nation and citizenry. The authors would like to express our deep appreciation for the IMLS as well as the University of Michigan Library for the sheer volume of its contribution of staffing, expertise, and hours. We would like to acknowledge the University of Michigan Library and the support of James Hilton, University Librarian and Dean of Libraries, and Donna Hayward, Associate University Librarian for Budget and Planning.

This project benefited from the ingenuity of many people who generously shared time and expertise in an overarching spirit of cooperation. It becomes a challenge to properly recognize all contributors for a project that involved many people over a span of nearly eight years. Over the years, several of the key personnel for CRMS moved from the University of Michigan to new opportunities. Their impact requires particular appreciation. John Wilkin conceived of CRMS and was the principal investigator for the first grant while at the University of Michigan Library as the Associate University Librarian for Library and Information Technology and as the founding Executive Director of HathiTrust. John is now the Dean of Libraries and University Librarian at University of Illinois at Urbana-Champaign. CRMS is John's brainchild. Paul Courant, Harold T. Shapiro Professor of Public Policy and Arthur F. Thurnau Professor in the Department of Economics and School of Information at the University of

ACKNOWLEDGMENTS

Michigan, provided key leadership as the Dean of Libraries at the University of Michigan from 2007 to 2013. Anne Karle-Zenith, now Digital Services Manager at METRO New York (the Metropolitan New York Library Council), had significant impact on shaping the structure, workflow, and relationships foundational to CRMS. Bobby Glushko, now head of Scholarly Communications and Copyright at University of Toronto Libraries, also played a vital role in the development of CRMS-World.

The Stanford Copyright Renewal Database, under the initiative of Mimi Calter, Associate University Librarian and Chief of Staff at Stanford University Libraries, closed a critical information gap and thus opened a window of possibility for tackling copyright indeterminacy. Kris Kasianovitz, also of Stanford University Libraries, and Bernadette Bartlett, Library of Michigan, helped shape our work on state government documents. An additional grant from the University of Michigan Library Creative Research fund supports an inquiry into our undetermined category of volumes, currently in process.

We would like to express our appreciation for the ongoing encouragement of a wide range of colleagues who have informally helped us think about copyright issues in the context of CRMS, including Nancy Kopans, Joyce Ray, John Mark Ockerbloom, Elizabeth Townsend Gard, Michael Seadle, Noam Solon, Robert Wolven, and Nancy Weiss. This toolkit benefitted from the careful reading and feedback of Ana Enriquez, Kyle Courtney, Greg Cram, Nazareth Pantaloni III, Laura Quilter, Erin Clements Rushing, Roger Schonfeld, and Hope O'Keeffe. We also want to express

ACKNOWLEDGMENTS

our deep appreciation to Allison Peters and Jason Colman from Michigan Publishing for their responsive and professional editorial guidance.

This endeavor would not have been possible without the collective commitment, support, and guidance of both the CRMS Advisory Working Group and the nineteen partner institutions that performed the daily work of CRMS. The commitment of CRMS partners took the form of precious staff time and the tireless dedication of individual reviewers. Projects like CRMS do not happen without enormous commitment—thousands of hours of work and dedicated staff time. The depth and breadth of the CRMS Advisory Working Group's expertise was crucial for checking our assumptions and shaping our processes; we were overwhelmed by the generosity and dedication of this exceptional group.

These acknowledgements can only partly speak to the foundational importance of shared, collaborative stewardship of the human record embodied in the work we have done through CRMS. In order to realize the potential of our shared collections, we must harness the energies of committed professionals like the ones who have made this endeavor successful.

UNIVERSITY OF MICHIGAN LIBRARY

Note that asterisks (*) in this section and beyond have been included to distinguish the names of key departments and personnel.

ACKNOWLEDGMENTS

U-M Library Copyright Office*

    Richard C. Adler, CRMS Project Manager
    Justin Bonfiglio, Copyright Specialist
    Kristina Eden, Copyright Outreach Librarian
    Melissa Levine, Lead Copyright Officer, Principal Investigator

U-M Digital Library Production Service—Library Information Technology

    Kat Hagedorn, Project Manager for Digital Projects
    John Weise, Manager, Digital Library Production Service*
    Perry Willett, Head, Digital Library Production Service, 2004–8

U-M Library Information Technology

    Brian "Moses" Hall, Applications Programmer / Analyst, Intermediate*
    Jose Blanco, Applications Programmer / Analyst, Senior
    Tom Burton-West, Applications Programmer / Analyst, Intermediate
    Aaron Elkiss, Systems Programmer / Analyst Senior
    Roger Espinosa, Applications Programmer / Analyst, Senior
    Phil Farber, Applications Programmer / Analyst, Senior
    Tim Prettyman, Applications Programmer / Analyst, Senior
    Jonathan Rothman, Head, Library Systems Office
    Josh Santelli, Applications Programmer / Analyst, Intermediate
    Cory Snavely, LIT Core Services Manager

ACKNOWLEDGMENTS

U-M Library Finance

    Eric Sortor, Senior Budget Analyst
    Hongyun Theros, Financial Specialist

U-M Technical Services

    Judith Ahronheim, Head, Electronic Resource Access Unit, Electronic Resources and Database Management Section*
    Matt Carruthers, Metadata Projects Librarian
    David Fulmer, Information Resources Assistant, Senior, 2008–11
    Senovia Guevara, Information Resources Assistant, Intermediate, 2009–10
    Martin Knott, Head, Electronic Resources and Database Management Section
    Dennis McWhinnie, Information Resources Assistant, Senior, Electronic Access Unit
    Greg Nichols, Electronic Resources Access Unit, Electronic Resources and Database Management Section*
    Emily Peiffer, Electronic Access Unit
    Eric Saran, Information Resources Assistant, Senior, 2008
    Heather Shoecraft, Information Resources, Senior
    Chris Wilcox, Information Resources Assistant, Senior, 2007–12

ACKNOWLEDGMENTS

HATHITRUST (BASED AT U-M)

Mike Furlough, Executive Director*
Melissa Stewart, Senior Administrative Assistant
Jeremy York, Assistant Director
Angelina Zaytsev, Project Librarian

CRMS ADVISORY WORKING GROUP

Jack Bernard, Associate General Counsel, University of Michigan
Kenneth D. Crews, Faculty Member, Columbia Law School; Of Counsel, Gipson Hoffman and Pancione
Sharon E. Farb, Associate University Librarian for Collections and Scholarly Communication, University of California, Los Angeles
Bobby Glushko, Head, Scholarly Communications and Copyright, University of Toronto Libraries
Georgia K. Harper, Scholarly Communications Advisor, University of Texas Libraries, University of Texas at Austin
Peter Hirtle, Affiliate Fellow, Berkman Center for Internet and Society, Harvard University
Jessica Litman, John F. Nickoll Professor of Law, University of Michigan Law School, and Professor of Information, University of Michigan School of Information
Kevin Smith, Director, Copyright and Scholarly Communication, Duke University Libraries

ACKNOWLEDGMENTS

PARTNERS: REVIEWERS AND LIAISONS

Baylor University Libraries

> Brenda Anderson, Ramona McKeown, Billie Peterson-Lugo, Denyse Rodgers, Jeff Steely, Darlene Youts

California Digital Library

> Ivy Anderson, Renata Ewing, Curtis Lavery, Nancy Scott-Noennig, Virginia Sinclair

University of California, Irvine

> Carol Hughes, Colby Riggs, Kevin Ruminson

University of California, Los Angeles

> Martin Brennan, Diane Gurman, Edward Kip Hannan, Angela Riggio

University of California, San Francisco

> Julia Kochi, David MacFarland

Columbia University Libraries

> Kaitlyn Burch, Ryan Graham, Zachary Lane, Robert Rendall

ACKNOWLEDGMENTS

Universidad Complutense de Madrid

>Antonio Moreno Cañizares, Almudena Caballos Villar

Dartmouth College Library

>Karla Bushway, Goodie Corriveau, Lori Heath, Judy Maynes, Sarah McBride, Jan Peltzer

Duke University Libraries

>Winston Atkins, Judith Bailey, Robert Byrd

University of Illinois at Urbana-Champaign Library

>Sarah Hoover, Betsy Kruger, Elizabeth Lippoldt, Hiromi Morikawa, Joshua Shelly, Angela Waarala

Indiana University Libraries

>Janet M. Black, Thomas Bullard, Lisa Cameron, Erin Green, Elizabeth Hanson, Kathryn Marlett, Sarah McAfoose, Jo McClamroch, Sherri Michaels, Nazareth Pantaloni III

Johns Hopkins University Library

>Christopher Case, Katherine DeSousa, Dawn Hale, Isabelle Kargon

ACKNOWLEDGMENTS

University of Maryland Libraries

Paul Bushmiller, Leigh Ann DePope, Donna King, Yeo-Hee Koh, Audrey Lengel, Terry Owen, Loretta Tatum

McGill University Library

Jennifer Innes, Louise Robert, Sarah Severson

University of Minnesota Library

Lynne Beck, Laureen Boutang, Sandra Cressman, Virginia Dudley, Steve Koehler, Dennis Lien, David Linton, Mary Mortenson, Rory Segety, Edward Swanson, Carla Urban, Mark Wilhelmi, Sue Zuriff

Northwestern University Library

Katie Brown, Ann Duncan-Gibbs, Liz Hamilton, Shelley Morrison, Dru Parrish, Claire Stewart, Jennifer Young, Dan Zellner

Ohio State University Library

Pamela Cale, Zaineb Bayahy, Sandra Enimil

ACKNOWLEDGMENTS

Penn State University Libraries

Ryan Ake, Benjamin Blakeslee-Drain, Carol Bridgens, Grace Brooks, Paula Contreras, Yesenia Figueroa-Lifschitz, Jonathan Hindman, Joseph Chris Holobar, Nicolle Nicastro, Jennifer Phillips, Melanie Rinker, Ann Snowman

Princeton University Library

Marvin Bielawski, Jennifer Block

University of Wisconsin-Madison Library

Michael Cohen, Cynthia Lundey, Maren Mayer, Lisa Nachreiner, Karen Rattunde, Rita Roemer, Alan Seeger, Henry Thompson, Irene Zimmerman

Introduction

ABOUT THE COPYRIGHT REVIEW MANAGEMENT SYSTEM TOOLKIT

This toolkit describes our effort to conduct copyright review of books at a large scale. As you read this toolkit, you may notice some things you would change. We encourage you to identify such opportunities for improvement. This project is the product of evolving tools, staff changes, policy, and practical day-to-day decisions. The CRMS toolkit is meant to make copyright review more accessible to anyone who chooses to take up this work, but it is not meant to circumscribe the activity.

We hope the methods developed here for CRMS will be adopted and adapted to help others responsibly identify and provide meaningful access to public domain collections. At the same time, we acknowledge that CRMS is only one approach in a portfolio of options available. There are many cases where copyright review will not be the preferred path for responsible stewardship of collections. Other provisions of copyright law—for example, fair use—provide robust frameworks that could be far more effective in a given context as you work to make your institution's collections more openly available. We encourage you to consider and evaluate these other options before embarking on a large-scale copyright review like CRMS. We also believe that aspects of the CRMS approach may be adopted for smaller projects.

In designing this toolkit, the project team relied on its personal experience with CRMS as well as the insights of reviewers, the Advisory Working Group, and HathiTrust stakeholders. We drew inspiration from a number

INTRODUCTION

of existing resources, including the IMLS-sponsored Digital Humanities Curation Guide.[1] We hope this toolkit will in turn inspire others working to expand the scope of CRMS activity.

Finally, we would like to note that CRMS processes have given us the latitude to conduct copyright review at a large scale with considerable independence from legal counsel—reducing the day-to-day burden on our counsel and moving our mission forward. While we hope that you will find this model useful, the methods expressed in this toolkit should not be considered legal advice. Ideally, this toolkit will be used as your core team works with your own legal counsel, especially as you develop the legal framework for your project. Once foundational principles are in place, the CRMS approach can help standardize workflow, achieve reliable results, and support the responsible stewardship of your collections.

---

1 "Digital Humanities Curation Guide," accessed January 21, 2016, http://guide.dhcuration.org.

Getting Started

HOW TO USE THIS TOOLKIT

This toolkit is divided into three main parts. It is primarily designed for copyright review of books, but it is also useful for a range of copyright review activities. The first part of the toolkit consists of a series of preplanning documents, one or more of which can be used in early-stage project meetings to build your team and plan your approach when faced with key questions. These documents are meant to help you decide who will be doing the work for your copyright review project and how they will be doing that work. Specifically, the preplanning section should help you

- assemble the team that you will be working with to perform copyright determinations
- identify the candidate volumes that you will be reviewing
- define your review process, workflow, and your project's desired outcomes
- build the case for your project to senior administrators

The second part of the toolkit dives deeper into the practical considerations facing a copyright review project, including project leadership, the legal fundamentals for copyright review, technical elements, and observations related to project personnel. We document many of the lessons learned over our years of CRMS activity and hope you will find this resource useful.

GETTING STARTED

Please note that before proceeding with this toolkit, you may be inclined to skim over the glossary, where we define key terms that will appear throughout the text.

The third part of the toolkit includes reports on pilot projects and a series of appendices. Together these form valuable documentation from the project. The pilot project reports detail discrete subprojects we explored through CRMS over the past several years. They are meant to provide a sense of both the opportunities and limitations of copyright review projects at scale. Topics covered include our experience piloting Spanish-language reviews, our efforts to improve name authority records (a useful by-product of our copyright review activity), and the expansion of CRMS activities to copyright-notice–based review of US state government documents. The appendices provide project resources that can serve as models or be repurposed for future projects.

Finally, we want this toolkit to be helpful, but we also aim to inspire a measure of caution. Copyright review, especially at scale, is challenging, and we want to be unambiguous about the difficulties associated with this work. If you are going to go down this path, we urge you to spend substantial time planning, to consider every tool and question we have identified in the preplanning portion of this toolkit, and to pilot your project before fully committing to a particular course of review activity. Your early-stage planning will pay substantial dividends over time.

GETTING STARTED

PREPLANNING DOCUMENT 1: BUILDING YOUR TEAM

CRMS evolved into a large-scale review project with nineteen partner institutions and more than sixty reviewers. Significant staff time was required for training and overseeing the work of those reviewers, as well as managing administrative requirements related to system security, access to digital scans, ongoing project documentation, and grant-based cost-share paperwork. The division of labor outlined in this document reflects the scale of CRMS. This document outlines five roles and recommends a minimum team of seven for larger projects. Your preplanning team should include a project manager and legal expert at the earliest stages, with additional roles added as the project develops. Smaller scale projects may be able to blend these roles and work with a smaller team. However, if your project grows in scale, it is important to consider the impact of that growth on staff resources.

1. Project Manager

Role Description

The project manager has overall responsibility for the project. The project manager is a liaison with HathiTrust (or other institutional administration) and ensures that formal requirements of the project are met and well documented. The project manager also works with the other team members to ensure that all component parts of the project are operating effectively.

GETTING STARTED

Key Considerations
- If working with HathiTrust, who on your team organizes the documentation required to facilitate reviewer access to digital scans, troubleshoots access as needed, and renews access on a regular basis?
- What documentation (monthly reports, project related memos, training materials) does your project require, and who is responsible for maintaining and archiving this documentation?
- Are there cost-share requirements or other financial reporting requirements for your grant? If yes, who is the liaison with partner institutions, ensuring that all relevant documents are collected and reported properly?

Additional Notes
Large-scale projects—especially multi-institution, grant-funded projects working with HathiTrust security protocols—generate significant, ongoing administrative work. Managing and accounting for work and documentation for cost-share commitments is complex. (For example, participants must understand if grants require that cost-share commitments are accounted for in dollar value of labor in contrast to effort/time alone.) Your team needs to consider this workload when planning.

2. Legal Expert

Role Description
The legal expert researches and identifies the legal considerations relevant to the project, then works with the project team to design the

GETTING STARTED

review process. The legal expert also oversees project development to ensure that it conforms to current law.

Key Considerations
- Does your project team have a dedicated copyright expert?
- What is the copyright expert's relationship with your institution's office of general counsel?
- Is the copyright expert's legal expertise sufficient for your proposed review project, or does your expert need to consult with others? If outside expertise is required, have you identified potential advisors?
- Do you have access to outside copyright expertise or oversight from an advisory group?
- Has one or more outside copyright experts verified your copyright review plan?
- After your project has started, how will you address new or unforeseen legal questions not covered in your initial planning documents?

Additional Notes
Copyright review projects present some legal risk, so your office of general counsel or equivalent should be made aware of your project and approve of your methods and workflow.

3. Developer

Role Description
The developer builds and maintains the online review interface, translates the legal framework into algorithms, adds new tools when available, and adapts and updates the system as needed. A dedicated developer is ideal, but some percentage of a developer's time is a minimum requirement for the duration of any rights research project relying on an online interface.

Key Considerations
- Are you using an online interface to manage all reviews?
- Have you consulted with a developer to anticipate future needs, based on your project's duration and potential evolution? What project changes, if any, do you anticipate over time?
- Who maintains the interface if software changes impede its operation?
- Who troubleshoots for you if the system goes down? How does system downtime affect the rest of your project plan?
- Have you identified a full-time or part-time developer who can dedicate considerable time to your project as needed?
- Has your developer reviewed the requirements for a copyright review management system as detailed in the technical section?

GETTING STARTED

Additional Notes

The CRMS project relies on the CRMS online interface detailed in the technical section of the toolkit. The interface required consistent development over time—new project tools emerged, outside changes (to HathiTrust or web browsers, for example) necessitated corresponding changes to the interface, and we explored new projects that also required adaptations of the interface.

4. Training and Reviewer Manager (Quality Control)

Role Description

Training and reviewer management are ongoing activities for large-scale review projects. Your project team should include at least one member focused on training reviewers and maintaining consistency in project execution.

Key Considerations

- Does your team have at least one point-person for communicating with and answering questions from reviewers? Who sets workflow policy as needs arise?
- Are your reviewers held to any performance standards requiring oversight?
- Do you provide ongoing training as needed or primarily at the beginning of the project?
- Do you anticipate reviewer turnover during the course of your project? How do you bring on new reviewers?

GETTING STARTED

> Do you have a plan for communicating with and updating all reviewers on any necessary changes?
>
> How do you document those changes over time in a way that reviewers and managers can reference and understand if they join the project after it has started?
>
> What training and assessment tools (i.e., video conferencing for remote reviewers, online quizzes, reviewer performance metrics) are available to your project team?

Additional Notes

If you have a small group of reviewers with little anticipated turnover, your project may require less oversight. Your project will require more consistent oversight and ongoing opportunities for reviewer training if you anticipate managing a growing number of reviewers over time, if reviewer turnover is expected on a regular basis, or if the project is relatively complex.

5. Copyright Reviewers

Role Description

The number of copyright reviewers will vary depending on the scale of your project. They perform the day-to-day copyright reviews, working directly with your project's candidate volumes and rendering copyright determinations for those volumes.

GETTING STARTED

Key Considerations
- How many reviewers work on the project? What is their time commitment? What is their hourly rate (dollar value of time committed based on salary) for accounting and cost-share purposes, if required?
- Do reviewers possess the language skills necessary to review the candidate pool?
- How do you add new reviewers to the project? Are reviewers removed from the project if they fail to meet certain objective requirements? When and how would you conduct such assessments?
- Do you have a set timeline for completing reviews? Is this timeline reasonable, given the number of reviewers and an approximation of the time required to review the types of volumes in your candidate pool?
- Have you identified expert reviewers (reviewers who can resolve conflicts in your review queue)? (A conflict occurs when two reviews for the same volume do not match.)

Additional Notes

Regardless of project scale, we recommend a minimum of three reviewers for any copyright review project, to allow for double review (see "Double Review" section).

GETTING STARTED

PREPLANNING DOCUMENT 2: BUILDING YOUR PROJECT

This set of questions is meant to help as you design your copyright review project. These questions may overlap with the previous preplanning document in this toolkit. Here they are framed within the context of the project, rather than by individual team roles. To better understand these questions, your project team should consult the body of the CRMS toolkit. Before undertaking a large-scale copyright review project, each of the following questions should be carefully considered and addressed.

Institutional Commitment

1. Does your institution's leadership understand the goals and risks of your project?
2. Has your institution's leadership approved your project?
3. Is your project funded and/or is staff time dedicated specifically to copyright review?
4. Is your institution's general counsel aware of your project and supportive?
5. Do you have access to a legal advisor familiar with copyright law?

Project Design

1. What is the primary goal of your project (e.g., identifying public domain volumes, collecting copyright-relevant information about volumes in your collection)?
2. What is the scope of your copyright review?

GETTING STARTED

   a. Are you reviewing books or some other kind of material, such as serials, sound recordings, or other media? Are you reviewing only one type of material or multiple types?
   b. What is the date range?
   c. Which countries of publication are involved? Are you targeting only one country or multiple countries?
   d. What languages are used in the material to be reviewed?
   e. Are there other particular features of the proposed collection that would have bearing on copyright determinations (e.g., publication status, contested or ambiguous applicable law)?

> In these preplanning questions, we reference nonbook materials (serials, sound recordings, or other media). To reiterate, this toolkit will be most helpful for the copyright review of book collections but can be used as an aid to planning for the copyright review of a wider range of materials.

3. What scope of access do you intend to provide to volumes you have reviewed (e.g., institution only, US-based access, worldwide access)?
4. Are you concerned about duplicative activity? Have you verified that the volumes you plan on reviewing are not already freely available online?

GETTING STARTED

5. If another copyright review project has reviewed similar volumes, what can you learn about their process to help improve your own reviews? Will you choose to accept their determinations, and how will you document that decision?
6. Have you identified the information you need to collect in order to make copyright determinations for your project (e.g., author death dates, US copyright renewal research)?
7. If you are basing your determinations on author death dates, have you identified the research tools (e.g., New General Catalog of Old Books & Authors [NGCOBA], Virtual International Authority File) you need to collect copyright-relevant information? If you are basing your copyright review on formalities, what tools do you plan on using (e.g., Stanford Copyright Renewal Database, Catalog of Copyright Entries, other)? (Note that the Stanford database consists almost exclusively of renewal records for books.)
8. What is your project timeline? Is it based on the number of volumes to be reviewed, institutional demands, or some other metric? Is it reasonable?

Data Collection

1. For volumes currently in copyright, are you collecting data sufficient for predicting when those volumes may enter the public domain?
2. Do your data collection methods consider future collection management and digitization decisions? For example, could your

GETTING STARTED

project easily identify authors whose works are likely to be in the public domain and then digitize accordingly?
3. Have you identified elements of bibliographic metadata that are likely to be useful for future searches and may be relevant for improving catalog records? Do you have a plan for encouraging reviewers to record these metadata in a consistent and uniform manner that will facilitate database search and retrieval?

Legal

1. What legal resources and personnel will you use to map out your copyright review process?
2. Have you identified a legal advisor who can provide feedback on your copyright review plan?
3. Are you basing your copyright review on past US copyright formalities (i.e., renewal and/or copyright notice)?
4. Have you accounted for copyright restoration in the United States due to the Uruguay Round Agreements Act (URAA), embodied in 17 U.S.C. § 104A?
5. If you are reviewing non-US publications, what resources and expertise will you draw on to understand the copyright laws of the relevant countries?
6. Are there categories of works that your project defines as unpublished? How do you make the determination that the works are unpublished? How does your project plan to determine the copyright status for these unpublished works?

GETTING STARTED

7. How will your project approach possible third-party authored content (inserts) within the volumes you review?
8. What facts (or lack of facts) will lead your reviewers to an "undetermined/need further investigation" determination for a given review?
9. If your project plans to make digital copies of volumes available as a result of your review, do you have a notice and takedown procedure in place?
10. Have you discussed this project with your institution's general counsel?

Project Management

1. How many reviewers will participate in your review project? Are they centrally located, or are they geographically dispersed?
2. How much time will each reviewer commit to the project per week?
3. What is the management structure of your review project?
4. Who will oversee reviewers? How will the project manager define expectations and monitor reviewers' accuracy and productivity levels? How will their issues be addressed?
5. Do reviewers have access to dedicated terminals in a secure, non-public area? Are they equipped with wide-screen monitors appropriate for reviewing digital scans of volumes?
6. How will you recognize and celebrate the contributions of the reviewers to the project?
7. What channels will you use to report and promote the progress of the project?

GETTING STARTED

Training

1. Will you consider adding new reviewers over time? If yes, who will train new reviewers?
2. Does your training plan include a "sandbox," where reviewers can practice on predetermined volumes?
3. What training materials and methods will you employ when bringing new reviewers onboard?
4. Do you have a performance threshold, below which reviewers will be retrained or removed from the project?
5. Do your training materials encourage uniformity and consistency in note-taking, especially for metadata terms that may be useful for searching the project database and making improvements to bibliographic metadata?

Process

1. Will your project employ a double-review system or will one reviewer's conclusion be determinative?
2. Do you have decision trees to guide reviewer behavior? Have you developed any other tools to help reviewers navigate the review process?
3. What is the full range of copyright determinations that can be made in your system? "Public domain"? "In copyright"? What else?
4. Are you using a "review interface" to make and track your determinations or are you using spreadsheets to perform this work?

GETTING STARTED

On June 18, 2013, HathiTrust joined the Digital Public Library of America (DPLA) as a formal partner and immediately became their largest content hub, ensuring a wide audience for the then-3.5 million public domain works in the HathiTrust collection. The partnership leveraged the strong support that the Institute of Museum and Library Services (IMLS) has shown for CRMS by also helping to cultivate the DPLA as it entered a critical period of high-profile promotion and expansion. Melissa Levine worked with DPLA on their cooperation with Europeana to develop cohesive rights metadata for DPLA and Europeana as aggregators. The resulting rights statements were in part influenced by CRMS and rights statements used by HathiTrust. For more information, see RightsStatements.org.

For large-scale projects, the development of an interface is very important, and this toolkit presumes you will work with a developer on your project. Our experience with using spreadsheets is that they are unwieldy and inefficient. Therefore we recommend against using them for long-term or large-scale projects.

Technical Considerations

1. Have you identified developer resources to support your project? Has your institution committed a dedicated developer to your project?
2. Has your institution committed the computational resources to serve a Web-based review interface and the database infrastructure to store review data? If stored data is lost, can it be restored from backup?
3. Can your institution guarantee a reasonable amount of system uptime to allow reviewers to work free of interruption? Does

GETTING STARTED

  your institution have support staff that can respond to an outage quickly?
4. Does your institution have the security infrastructure to prevent unauthorized access to the system and the scans?

Verification

1. Do you have quality control methods built into your process, like a double-review system?
2. Will you work with a third party to independently check a given number of your results? If yes, what is your procedure for an external check?
3. If an external check provides useful information related to your review process, what is your plan for integrating that information into your process?

Funding

1. How is your project work being funded?
2. If your work is funded through a grant, what are the reporting requirements of the grant? What documentation do you need to collect? What are the important grant deadlines that your team members need to be aware of?
3. If your work is funded through a multipartner cost-share grant, can your partners maintain the cost-share commitment if key project personnel depart?

GETTING STARTED

4. Does your institution have a plan for sustaining the work after the end of the grant period?
5. What are the long-term costs for sustaining your review project?

PREPLANNING DOCUMENT 3: CRMS PROJECT DECISION POINTS

This list is meant to guide new project planners through the key decision points for their copyright review project. Over the years, we have found that the following questions must be addressed when undertaking copyright review of books at scale. Planning how your project team intends to treat categories of work (e.g., translations, dissertations, dictionaries) will help you allocate reviewer resources more effectively and understand the research tools you will need to reach a determination.

This list is drawn from our experience working primarily with book collections in CRMS-US and CRMS-World. It is meant to be illustrative for all project planners but is most helpful for book review projects. While we focus on book collections in this list of considerations, there are analogous considerations for other materials.

Please describe in detail how your project will treat the following copyright-related issues:

GETTING STARTED

Foreign Language/Script

How will your reviewers work with volumes in foreign languages? Does your project have a mechanism for referring foreign language volumes to a reviewer with the relevant language proficiency, or will your project disregard foreign language volumes?

Inserts

Do you expect your reviewers to look for the presence of third-party authored materials in volumes they review? If so, how much scrutiny do you expect your reviewers to apply? How will your reviewers treat the presence of third-party authored materials incorporated into a volume being reviewed? What does or does not count as an insert?

Translations

When a work is identified as a translation (or contains translations), what guidance do you provide reviewers?

Dissertation/Thesis

Will your review project treat dissertations or theses differently from other published works? In what ways will you treat them differently?

Periodicals

If your project team will review periodicals, how will you identify third-party authored content in the periodicals? What assumptions are you making regarding works made for hire?

Non–Class A Works (United States)

Most books published in the United States between 1923 and 1963 are referred to as "Class A" works by the US Copyright Office. Renewal records for these books can be searched in the Stanford Copyright Renewal Database. Non–Class A works include serials, artwork, photographs, screenplays, and works prepared for oral delivery. We have found that renewal records for non–Class A works are harder to research due to the absence of a resource like the Stanford Copyright Renewal Database. If your project is based on the presence or absence of a copyright renewal for US works, will you extend your project to non–Class A works? If yes, how do you intend to do this?

Editions

Does your project address the possibility of variable copyright terms for multiple editions of a work?

GETTING STARTED

Government Works

What guidance will you provide to reviewers for identifying a government work, such as Crown copyright for Commonwealth countries?

Author-Based Determinations

For projects that base copyright determinations on the death date of the author of the work (as opposed to formalities, including US copyright renewal and notice requirements), how will your project treat the following categories of works?

- Known author
- Known (multiple) authors
- Uncertain or conflicting death dates for known authors
- Unknown/anonymous author(s)
- Corporate authors
- Government works
- Unpublished works

GETTING STARTED

At a Glance—Overview

The ideas expressed in this overview are meant to be a brief introduction to the topics more fully described later in the main toolkit. With that said, we think the simple principles found in this overview should be foundational to any copyright review project. Later we will show you how we work these principles into our daily practice.

LEADERSHIP

If you are reviewing the copyright status of a set of published books in your collection, you'll first want to make certain that your institution's leaders are aligned with your proposed project. Several key questions must be answered before you move forward, including the following:

1. *Is funding or a dedicated percentage of employee time available for and committed to the review project?* Without a financial commitment from the institution or from some external funding source, copyright review at any scale is impossible. The greater the scale of your review project, the greater the financial commitment required—for review projects shared across multiple institutions, project administration costs can be significant.
2. *Are administrators and your institution's office of general counsel aware of your project and supportive?* Making a copyright determination and implementing it requires a degree of legal risk for your institution. For example, if your review determines that a work is in the public domain, and your institution makes it available online,

AT A GLANCE—OVERVIEW

the risk is that one or more rights holders will disagree with the determination and threaten to bring suit. While in many cases the risk is low, your institution's leadership must be willing and able to evaluate and accept the risk.

3. *What are your project's time constraints, and what resources are available for its evolution?* In any institution with competing priorities, resource commitment questions are extremely important. Institutional leadership should clearly communicate whether the project is bounded by a specific set of goals or if it is meant to continue, change, and adapt over time.

PROJECT SCOPING

Proper project scoping is the single most important thing you can do to ensure that you are putting your project resources to their best use. Your project's scope defines the pool of works you choose to review and must be intimately tied to your project's goals.

For example, if one of your goals is to maximize public domain determinations, you would not want to review works published in the United States after 1989. Copyright renewal and notice were not required for US

AT A GLANCE—OVERVIEW

works published after 1989; with limited exceptions, the vast majority of post-1989 works will not have entered the public domain.[2]

Similarly, if you are seeking to identify public domain works under the copyright law of the UK, you are far less likely to identify public domain works published after the current year minus seventy years. UK copyright law protects a single-author book published by a UK author for seventy years after the author's death. Unless it was published posthumously, a book published in 1950 would be protected by copyright in the UK until at least 2021. It would therefore not make sense for a UK-centric copyright review project to focus on 1950s books at this time.

For US-based copyright determinations for books, we have found that the most fruitful publication date range for making copyright determinations is 1923–63, during which time many works entered the public domain due to failure to adhere to US copyright formalities. For non-US determinations, we tend to map our candidate volumes to the relevant country's copyright duration. Again, given that an author of a work is usually alive when the work is first published, we currently do not review UK works published after the current year minus seventy years (UK is a "life + 70" regime; for example, 1944 + 70 = 2014. Works published by authors who died in 1944 entered the public domain in the UK on January 1, 2015).

---

2 This insight is likely to be true until at least 2059. Here, a notable exception would be US federal government works. See 17 U.S.C. § 105 ("Copyright protection under this title is not available for any work of the United States Government").

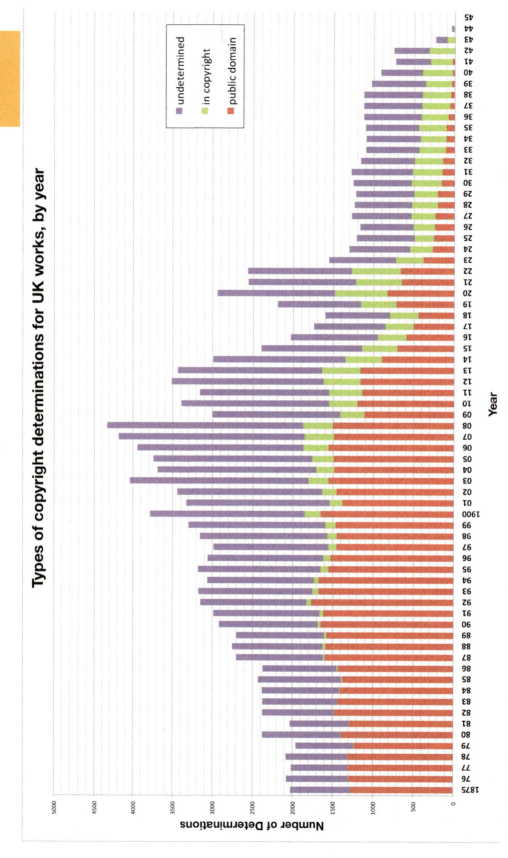

Figure 1 Breakdown of public domain, in-copyright, and undetermined works, published in the United Kingdom, 1875–1944

AT A GLANCE—OVERVIEW

LEGAL

A full understanding of the copyright laws of the jurisdictions relevant to your project is essential to any copyright review system. For a fuller understanding of the legal analysis and research that we have undertaken, see the full legal section in the main body of this toolkit.

To research US copyright law, we have drawn heavily on resources including current and past US Copyright Acts, Peter Hirtle's *Copyright Term and the Public Domain in the United States* chart,[3] the US Copyright Office's Circulars,[4] and copyright treatises like *Nimmer on Copyright*.[5]

For international legal regimes, our primary resources have been Geller and Nimmer's *International Copyright Law and Practice*[6] and the text of specific intellectual property laws and treaties available through the

---

[3] Peter Hirtle. "Copyright Term and the Public Domain in the United States," last modified January 3, 2016, http://copyright.cornell.edu/resources/publicdomain.cfm.

[4] US Copyright Office. "Circulars and Brochures," accessed January 20, 2016, http://copyright.gov/circs/.

[5] Melville B. Nimmer and David Nimmer. *Nimmer on Copyright* (New York: Matthew Bender, 1978–).

[6] Paul Edward Geller and Melville B. Nimmer. *International Copyright Law and Practice* (Newark, NJ: Matthew Bender, 2009).

World Intellectual Property Organization's WIPO Lex.[7] These resources have been essential for the work we have done to date. For specific international legal regimes that are not covered by these resources, your project team should explore working with translators and copyright experts specializing in the specific copyright laws related to your project.

PERSONNEL

CRMS benefited from having a centralized core staff able to manage the large-scale copyright review being performed by decentralized reviewers at our nineteen partner institutions. Our core staff included a project manager, a trainer, a copyright specialist, and a primary developer. Project administration, development, and system maintenance all require substantial oversight and must be performed by a management team.

Beyond personnel dedicated to overseeing a project, your project must have reviewers who are patient and detail oriented, can dedicate five to ten hours per week to the practice of copyright review, and are interested in and willing to work with the nuances of copyright law. We have found that debate and discussion is important to this process; resources permitting, copyright review should not be the work of a single individual.

---

7 World Intellectual Property Organization. "WIPO Lex," accessed January 20, 2016, http://www.wipo.int/wipolex/en/.

AT A GLANCE—OVERVIEW

If your project is to grow in size, you must identify reviewers who share the traits listed above, are willing to learn and follow set protocols, and can commit weekly hours to the project (so their review skills do not atrophy). Ideally, your review project will have the flexibility to substitute new reviewers over time as individual and institutional priorities shift. Project planning should include a method for accommodating staff changes in the project team over time.

The evolution of the copyright review system may also inform personnel choices. If your project begins to take on non-English languages, for example, support from reviewers fluent in those languages would be ideal. Alternatively, working with language experts and training English-language reviewers may be effective. Thus far, we have had some success in piloting Spanish-language reviews. Some languages, such as Chinese or Russian, would demand collaboration with a committed team of language experts.

A rights determination project like the one discussed here requires significant and ongoing technical resources, including a rights review interface, a database, and staff sufficiently skilled to support them. For this reason, we strongly recommend having a full-time developer devoted to the project.

In some cases, it is probably best that your team leaves the copyright review of specific works to a different or future set of reviewers. Knowing when you are not the ideally suited reviewer for a job is important; identifying the right person or institution and collaborating with them is the best way to address some copyright review challenges. Ultimately, we would like to see copyright review work shared more broadly, with one set of reviewers performing the reviews and another verifying the results, validating them, and ultimately facilitating access decisions for partner institutions.

COPYRIGHT REVIEW

The main focus of a copyright review for a book is answering one question: Is any part of this book still protected by copyright? We tend to ask this question first at the volume level, but we are also sensitive to in-copyright elements contained within the body of the book.

You can perform a copyright review with the physical book in front of you, but we do not recommend this if you intend to perform copyright reviews at scale. Our reviewers often review hundreds of titles in a given week; doing this with physical copies is incredibly inefficient and introduces significant logistical challenges. From our perspective, being able to use digital scans for copyright determinations is essential to large-scale copyright review.

AT A GLANCE—OVERVIEW

Resources like the Stanford Copyright Renewal Database[8] and the Virtual International Authority File[9] (VIAF) are foundational tools for copyright review. In the United States, renewal of copyright was a requirement for works published from 1923 to 1963; we use the Stanford Copyright Renewal Database to look for the presence or absence of a renewal record for books published in this time range. International legal regimes are generally based on the life of the author plus a set number of years (for instance, the UK adds seventy years; Canada adds fifty). Identifying the death date of the author(s) of a work is central to determining its copyright status in these regimes.

Our copyright review outcomes can be generalized into three broad categories: "public domain," "in copyright," and "und/nfi" (undetermined/needs further investigation). The und/nfi category gives reviewers an option when a copyright review is too complex or is likely to be indeterminate based on the resources available. Large-scale copyright review requires practical, flexible features to promote efficiency; for CRMS, the und/nfi category is one such feature.

---

8 Stanford University Libraries & Academic Information Resources. "Copyright Renewal Database," accessed January 20, 2016, http://collections.stanford.edu/copyrightrenewals/.

9 Online Computer Library Center. "The Virtual International Authority File," accessed January 20, 2016, http://viaf.org.

AT A GLANCE—OVERVIEW

DOCUMENTATION

We document our copyright research as thoroughly as possible but in a way that is streamlined and does not excessively burden our reviewers. The interface provides standard rights and reason codes so that reviewers may select them with minimal additional work. We also provide reviewers with a free-text notes field, so that they may log any additional information relevant to their copyright review. To the degree possible, we encourage uniformity in our codes and notes fields; uniformity is key to searching and studying the historical data generated by our reviews.

Our documentation serves as a foundation for our copyright determinations. It provides us with a basis for verifying our results, tracking the research that went into any given determination, and reappraising work if new information becomes available or if we wish to perform deeper research on a specific category of works.

For example, we often mark works with probable anonymous authors (works where it is not possible by reasonable inquiry to ascertain the identity of the author) as undetermined and advise reviewers to add "anonymous" to the free text notes field. We do this because it is frequently very difficult to confirm that an author is anonymous rather than simply hard to identify. If we later decide to perform a deeper review of these anonymous works, perhaps to determine whether the anonymous authors have been identified, we can search for those works where we've made the "anonymous" note.

AT A GLANCE—OVERVIEW

OUTPUT/ACCESS DECISIONS

Rights determinations translate into public access online, and making access decisions in accordance with your rights review should be mapped out at an early stage in your copyright review project. Ideally, we recommend this be done in collaboration between rights reviewers and developers of the platform being used for access. Failure to do this could result in inefficiencies and repeated efforts later in the process.

Access based on our copyright determinations generally falls into the following three groups: (1) access to the work within the United States; (2) access worldwide; and (3) access to the work outside of, but not within, the United States. The third category of access—access to works outside of (but not within) the United States—is due to the possibility of copyright restoration, which we will detail more fully in the main CRMS Toolkit. For now, suffice it to say that the concept of the public domain may vary from country to country. For example, in some cases, works that have entered the public domain in their country of origin are still under copyright in the United States due to copyright restoration.

VERIFICATION

Individual errors are difficult to avoid, and some form of verification should be a part of your copyright review.

AT A GLANCE—OVERVIEW

Our baseline quality control method is a double-review system: Two reviewers review each book in CRMS independently. Their reviews are then compared; if the reviews match, the review is accepted by the system. If they do not match, an expert reviewer adjudicates the reviews and comes to a final determination. This system helps us minimize the impact of individual human errors that should be expected in any review project.

In the CRMS Toolkit, we will discuss third-party verification of copyright reviews. We believe that working with third parties is an important means of checking and refining your copyright review project—ideally, an independent review will show that your system is functioning well and in alignment with the law. A third-party review is a valuable means of making sure that you have developed processes that gird the integrity of your project.

FUNDING

Copyright review requires time. The more complex your reviews become, the more time, human resources, and funding will be required. A single-author book written between 1923 and 1963 with absolutely no content other than the author's main text is a pretty simple proposition for copyright review. Serials, newspapers, and other more complex copyright objects often demand deeper study. A movie containing sound recordings (each with their own layers of rights), an underlying script, and moving images will typically require a substantial expenditure of resources to review; funding for complex copyright review projects should be calibrated accordingly.

If your institution wants to take on complexity, we celebrate you. At the same time, we would caution that, in addition to higher costs, some of the tools our CRMS reviewers rely on (e.g., Stanford Copyright Renewal Database) were not developed for more complex copyright objects. To date, a fully searchable database of the Catalog of Copyright Entries has not been developed. Searching through the CCE to discover nonbook registrations and renewals can be laborious, time-consuming, and consequently expensive.

Your funding source will also impact your project's ability to make changes throughout its course. The very generous IMLS grants supporting CRMS work have been absolutely essential to the success of CRMS, and we are deeply grateful for the support we have received. At the same time, managing cost-share partners made it difficult to repurpose reviewers and modify our goals as we moved through the grant period. Managing cost-share reports and communicating with a large number of reviewers and participating institutions also present administrative costs. These should be factored into the project budget or funding proposal.

AT A GLANCE—
OVERVIEW

Involving Your Leadership

Questions of institutional liability and risk tolerance emerge where copyright is involved. For this reason, keeping channels of communication open between decision makers and institutional leaders is important. Open communication helps ensure that a project does not diverge substantially from community-accepted norms and practices. It also creates opportunities to draw on the good guidance and experience of leaders who may have faced similar decisions before.

DEAN AND LIBRARY ADMINISTRATORS

Your institution's senior leadership should be engaged in the decision to embark on a large-scale copyright review (for CRMS, this means the university librarian and dean of libraries at the University of Michigan Library). A dean of libraries or equivalent leader ought to be made aware of your project before approving it and should be apprised of any significant course corrections throughout the project's timeline.

The reasons to secure high-level approval from your institution are straightforward. First, proper copyright review at any scale is a significant investment of resources, and institutional leaders must be ready and willing to allocate proper resources to the activity. If there is no financial commitment in the form of funding or dedicated staff hours, then any copyright review project is unlikely to meet its objectives. Second, as copyright review is a human endeavor, mistakes in copyright determinations are inevitable, and course corrections are occasionally necessary. Therefore, it is important that leaders never be blindsided by your activities; instead, they ought to be well informed about any legal risks your project may present. Finally, informed leaders can be more effective advocates for your project. They can spread the word about your work, opening doors for potentially valuable collaborations.

However, we do not advocate for overinvolving the highest leaders of your institution. CRMS does not engage the dean of libraries in most of the daily operations of the project—we communicate big-picture activities and changes, make our human resource needs known to library administrators, and communicate the reasonable limits of what can be accomplished with the resources available to us.

OFFICE OF GENERAL COUNSEL

For our purposes, alignment and frequent, frank communication with the Office of General Counsel is crucial to the overall success of CRMS. A general counsel can help a copyright determination project consider process, recalibrate (if necessary), and check assumptions against reasonable and good-faith standards. Our relationship with general counsel is an important asset to the CRMS process, and any institution intending to embark on large-scale copyright review should recognize the importance of good counsel for this process.

If your institution lacks counsel well versed in copyright law, you will want to seriously consider your options for securing an advisor who can align legal analysis with tempered, institution-level judgment.

INVOLVING YOUR LEADERSHIP

Institutions facing this issue should consider the formation of an advisory group (detailed below).

HATHITRUST LEADERSHIP

Although CRMS works closely with HathiTrust (also hosted at the University of Michigan), administratively it is a separate project. HathiTrust implements CRMS copyright determinations, and it is ultimately HathiTrust leadership that decides how to interpret and execute the determinations CRMS reviewers make. HathiTrust leadership establishes and enforces strict security protocols related to its digital volumes, facilitates access to HathiTrust collections whenever legally permissible, and is the final authority on all collections-related decision making.

Since its inception, CRMS has been closely aligned with HathiTrust and its leadership. Our working relationships with HathiTrust's executive director and Rights and Access Working Group have been vital to the success of the project.[10] The collaborative environment of HathiTrust has also informed the structure of CRMS. Our reviewers have historically been members of the HathiTrust community, and the success of CRMS is a direct result of multi-institutional collaboration. While CRMS is an

---

10 For more information on HathiTrust governance, see HathiTrust, "Our Partnership," accessed January 20, 2016, https://www.hathitrust.org/partnership.

independent project, our mission has meshed well with the values and needs of HathiTrust and its members.

ADVISORY WORKING GROUP

Copyright review is often complex. An advisory group of copyright experts can provide historical context, help to avoid pitfalls or flawed logic, and connect your project with much-needed expertise. Even copyright experts may disagree on interpretations of current law, so having a range of experienced opinions will help to ensure that issues are addressed from a variety of perspectives.

The CRMS Advisory Working Group was formed in 2011 as a key part of the second National Leadership Grant from the IMLS to support CRMS. This working group offers recommendations related to CRMS processes, assists in validating our legal analysis, identifies areas for improvement, and works through related areas of inquiry. The members volunteer their time and expertise, offer regular feedback through e-mail correspondence, and provide general policy direction and recommendations in areas of first impression.

Project Scoping

Project scoping is critical to the success of a copyright determination project. Proper scoping helps

- avoid confusion that could result from juggling multiple legal regimes within one project
- identify the research tools and human resources that will be necessary to meet the project's goals
- facilitate the creation of a manageable review process by reducing the number of variables required to make a determination

A properly scoped project will allow you to make the most effective use of your available resources. For example, if your primary goal was to identify works in the public domain, it would be unproductive to design a copyright review project around post-1989 US publications. In some cases, a line can be drawn without need for individual copyright review (a well-known example is pre-1923 publications in the United States.) Similarly, in our experience, virtually all works published more than 140 years ago can be properly considered public domain worldwide without review.

THE SCOPE OF CRMS-US

A volume was a candidate for CRMS-US if it matched the following criteria:

PROJECT SCOPING

- Rights status of "ic/bib" ("in copyright by virtue of bibliographic data," a default status assigned by the system based on bibliographic metadata)
- Bibliographic format of "bk" (book)
- Published between 1923 and 1963
- Published in the United States (i.e., not a foreign work)
- Written in English
- Not a US federal government document
- Not a translation
- Not a dissertation

For CRMS-US, we focused on reviewing books published 1923–63 in the United States for the following reasons:

- Books were the focus of our review in order to leverage the Stanford Copyright Renewal Database, a resource geared toward "Class A" materials (mainly books), without which a review of a book would currently be a much slower proposition.
- Published works were important because unpublished works may receive a different copyright term and further research is often required when there is an underlying question regarding publication.
- 1923–63 (inclusive) was the time range when US copyright law required renewal of copyright.[11] If a work was first published in the

---

11 The starting point for any US-based review project is 1923 because we treat all works published prior to 1923 as in the public domain under US law. The end point for a

United States during this time period but not renewed twenty-eight years after publication, then it is properly considered to have entered the public domain for the purposes of US law.

IDEAS FOR REFINING A CANDIDATE POOL

There are two key ways in which the candidate pool could be filtered to remove (or at least flag) works that have a high probability of being in copyright. The first would be to run an automatic query (author, title) of the candidate volume catalog records against the Stanford Copyright Renewal Database. Any works that match would be very likely to be in copyright and could be removed from the candidate pool. (This presumes that your cataloging system and the Stanford Copyright Renewal Database can be reliably matched. Your technical support will need to perform appropriate tests to confirm that this will be possible.)

The second filtering method is matching non-US authors listed in the Virtual International Authority File (VIAF) with the authors listed in the catalog record for the purposes of identifying works where copyright restoration may be applicable. The presence of a non-US author in the catalog record alone does not necessarily mean that copyright restoration applies, but it does flag cases where non-US authorship may complicate the review process. See the legal section for more on copyright restoration.

---

review project based on renewal is 1963, because any work published on or after January 1, 1964, was not subject to the renewal requirement.

THE SCOPE OF CRMS-WORLD

A volume was a candidate for CRMS-World if it matched the following criteria:

- Rights status of "ic/bib" or "pdus/bib" ("public domain US only"; both are default statuses assigned by the system based on bibliographic metadata)
- Published in Australia, Canada, or the UK
- Published between the following spans (see paragraph below)
  - 1873–1943 (UK)
  - 1893–1963 (Australia or Canada)
- Written in English
- Not a translation
- Single publication/copyright date

When CRMS-World was developed, we decided to focus on volumes first published in the UK, Canada, and Australia. We did this for the following three practical reasons:

- For the relevant date range, these three countries represented a candidate pool of appropriate scale: approximately 170,000 works fell into this category
- They were English-language works, which promised to make the review process less complicated for our US-based reviewers
- The legal regimes of these three countries were sufficiently similar to form a coherent project

PROJECT SCOPING

CRMS review projects, including any review encompassed by CRMS-World, do not consider works published more than 140 years ago. Because international copyright terms typically persist for the life of the author plus a defined number of years after the author's death, we consider 140 years as an appropriate threshold. Here is our logic: a hypothetical twenty-year-old author writing and publishing in the UK in 1875 would need to have lived to age ninety (1945) for their work to still be in copyright in the UK in 2016. If that same author were twenty-five when publishing in 1875, they would need to have lived to age ninety-five for the same to be true, with more remote scenarios emerging for older authors publishing in 1875.

On the other end of the spectrum, CRMS-World does not currently review UK works published after 1944. We made this decision because the UK bases its copyright duration for most published books on the life of the author plus seventy years. A book published in 1945, where the author died that very year, would be protected until January 1, 2016 (1945 + 70 = end of 2015). From our perspective, it is likely that authors survived the publication of their books by a few years. We sought to maximize our resources by focusing on reviews of books more likely to be in the public domain.

We arrived at our 140-year rolling wall using the hypothetical twenty-year-old author example, described above. Your project team may decide this is too liberal or too conservative an approach. This is a policy decision, and your project team should evaluate it independently.

Additionally, your project team should consider further refinement of the tail end of your candidate pool. Here, you could study the number of public domain determinations for works published after set dates. How many works published in 1942 have entered the public domain due to the author's death date? Published in 1941? Published in 1937? If you find a high percentage of these works are in copyright due to author death date, it may behoove you to review earlier publication date ranges. Here, we note that the collection of relevant death date information can serve predictive purposes and is important even without a public domain determination. If you agree with this view, then capping your publication date for review may not be necessary.

Finally, working with a catalog record, you could decide to filter out any works featuring listed authors who died after a specific date (1946, for example). This would eliminate the need to review works that would definitely be adjudicated "in copyright" in a present-day review.

AN ALTERNATE APPROACH: AUTHOR-BASED SCOPING

Though we did not implement it in CRMS, we did consider the potential benefits of an "author-based" approach to copyright review.

The central data point for most non-US copyright determinations is the death date of the author. With a death date, a reviewer could easily make a copyright determination for anything written and published by a given author. From our perspective, scoping your candidate pool to include only works for which an author and death date are known would be more efficient, given that reviewers would not have to approach each work by the same author "fresh" each time.

The challenge with any author-based approach is that books often contain contributions from multiple authors, so your project must be sensitive to the possibility that a given author death date may not be determinative for all works in which that author has contributed material.

With the above caveat recognized, we believe that a properly designed author-based approach may yield substantial gains in efficiency. We also find that an author-based approach lends itself to the identification of high-return death-date research projects. When an author is tied to many works, and his or her death date cannot be located, that information gap can prevent a large number of copyright determinations. Arguably, when we know that the identification of an author death date would provide clarity for a great number of volumes, investing the resources to locate that death date becomes worthwhile.

The identification of an author's death date is central to copyright determinations for that author's work. One byproduct of our research has been the collection of new death date information, which we contribute to cataloging efforts whenever possible. We believe this activity has great potential, and we would be pleased to see the emergence of a more organized program in support of author death date research.

ANOTHER APPROACH FOR US WORKS: COPYRIGHT NOTICE-BASED REVIEW

In the United States, affixing a copyright notice on a published work was a formal requirement of the law until March 1, 1989. From January 1, 1978 through March 1, 1989, failure to affix notice to the work could be remedied by registering copyright in the work within five years.[12] Prior to 1978, however, this remedy was not available—virtually all pre-1978 US works published without a copyright notice entered the public domain by operation of law.

At an early stage, we made the policy decision for CRMS not to review volumes for the presence or absence of a copyright notice alone. Instead, for two related reasons, CRMS-US focused on renewal records in the review process. First, the early planners of CRMS-US saw value

---

12 Peter Hirtle. "Copyright Term and the Public Domain in the United States," last modified January 3, 2016, http://copyright.cornell.edu/resources/publicdomain.cfm.

in leveraging the Stanford Copyright Renewal Database for identifying renewal records. Stanford could be searched quickly and efficiently, making it an ideal tool for copyright determination research and one that nearly matched the speed of checking for a copyright notice in the work itself. Our second concern was the possibility that the scans we were reviewing for our determinations might have had missing pages. This conservative stance was taken to reduce the likelihood of mistakes, and it is one that has resulted in arguably fewer public domain determinations. Today, we have greater confidence in the quality and completeness of scans, lending support to copyright review of US works based primarily on the presence or absence of copyright notice.

APPLICATION: US STATE GOVERNMENT DOCUMENTS

Our work with US state government documents is one example of scoping a project around the copyright notice formality. Copyright notice review allows reviewers to focus on the volume alone and does not require extensive use of additional research tools.

Our focus on US state government documents is based on a recognized need. Researchers from other institutions depend on state banking reports and similar state documents to perform valuable historical research. It is also based on evidence that many states often did not intend to assert copyright in their publications. When a publicly supported state government document was published without a copyright notice during the time range when the copyright law required such a notice, we see a good opportunity for review.

With regard to US state government documents, the presence or absence of copyright notice is sufficient to make public domain determinations for volumes published from 1923 to 1977. Arguably, review for the presence or absence of notice could be applied to state government documents through 1989, but a project reviewing through 1989 would risk a possible uptick in the number of works that did not bear a copyright notice but were registered within the five-year window.[13]

---

13 This risk could be mitigated by adding a check for post-publication registration via the post-1978 records in the US Copyright Office's Online Catalog.

Legal

ABOUT THIS LEGAL SECTION

This legal section is geared toward librarians, archivists, and decision makers at their respective institutions. It is meant to highlight and explain many of the legal issues that the CRMS team has grappled with over the past several years. CRMS represents a multiyear investment in mapping US and international copyright laws to the practice of making large-scale copyright determinations for book collections. If your project hopes to do similar work or sustain CRMS in the future, this section contains many of the legal factors your project team should consider.

Whenever possible, we provide concrete examples of the practical issues facing large-scale digital library projects. We will provide context to some of the tough decisions that memory institutions must resolve as they take on new projects. You may disagree with individual positions we take, and you may have a different set of priorities. This section should serve as a point of reference, a starting point for institution-specific discussion, analysis, and decision making.

If your institution is planning to take on a copyright-related project, your team should include at least one member who is willing and able to grapple with the legal issues intrinsic to any project involving copyright. Ideally, that person will be able to draw on the experience and guidance of others with copyright expertise—for us, this additional guidance comes from the CRMS Advisory Working Group. Your project team's ability to reasonably navigate copyright law will help minimize mistakes and reduce the liability of your institution. Here, as always, we emphasize the

LEGAL

importance of acting in good faith. Being a reasonable actor does not absolutely eliminate risk, but it will be a factor in your favor if a decision you have made is challenged.

Given that your project should involve one or more copyright experts, this legal section should help those experts better navigate the complexity involved in copyright review, identify useful tools and resources to confront tough questions, and build a framework for copyright review that meshes with your institution's aspirations, mission, and tolerance for risk. We also provide relevant legal resources that should be consulted for a deeper understanding of the topics discussed in this section.

CRMS-US: BUILDING COPYRIGHT EXPERTISE

The legal foundation of CRMS-US is based on the current US Copyright Act (as codified in Title 17 of the US Code), the 1909 Copyright Act, an understanding of the history of copyright and its evolution in the United States, and a familiarity with copyright-relevant case law.

There is a cornucopia of information related to US copyright law, and your copyright expert will need to have access to legal resources and engage with them. Multivolume treatises like *Nimmer on Copyright*, online resources like those found at Stanford's Copyright and Fair

LEGAL

Use Center,[14] Copyright Office Circulars,[15] and law journal articles available through databases like HeinOnline are a few key examples of the resources available to address the copyright issues you will face. This section details essential CRMS-related copyright concepts but is no substitute for deeper study and reference to these resources.

Case law relevant to copyright can be a moving target. While treatises and resources that distill and comment on the law are vital, we believe that your copyright expert should also be willing and able to engage the text of the Copyright Act and the legal decisions that have interpreted it. Your copyright expert must be familiar with resources like LexisNexis and Westlaw and should be able to Shepardize or KeyCite cases within these legal databases.

Beyond expertise, your institution should be prepared to commit resources to your copyright project, up to and including subscription fees to appropriate legal references. While a great deal of material is now freely available online, having access to a nearby law library streamlined our research and was a vital additional resource for the CRMS team.

---

14 Stanford University Libraries. "Copyright and Fair Use," accessed January 20, 2016, http://fairuse.stanford.edu.

15 US Copyright Office. "Circulars and Brochures," accessed January 20, 2016, http://copyright.gov/circs/.

DURATION OF COPYRIGHT IN THE US

Today, US copyright subsists in an original work of authorship from the moment it is fixed in a tangible medium of expression.[16] It endures for the life of the author plus seventy years.[17] This was not always the case. US law required copyright notice and renewal of copyright for much of the twentieth century. If a rights holder did not adhere to US copyright formalities, their work entered the public domain.

Peter Hirtle's *Copyright Term and the Public Domain in the United States* provides an extraordinarily useful reference for the varied US copyright terms enjoyed by copyright holders in the United States.[18] The CRMS-US project was based on the copyright renewal requirement, a formality required for US copyright through the end of 1963. If a work first published with notice in 1963 were properly renewed, the copyright term would have been ninety-five years from publication of the work. If not renewed in the twenty-eighth year after its publication, that work entered the US public domain.[19].

---

16 17 U.S.C. § 102(a).

17 17 U.S.C. § 302(a).

18 Peter Hirtle. "Copyright Term and the Public Domain in the United States," last modified January 3, 2016, http://copyright.cornell.edu/resources/publicdomain.cfm.

19 There is a split in the mechanics of the 1909 renewal requirement that took effect January 1, 1950. For works published prior to January 1, 1950, renewal was required in the year preceding the 28th anniversary of publication; for works published after

LEGAL

Also worth highlighting is the Samuelson Law, Technology and Public Policy Clinic's valuable handbook, *Is It in the Public Domain?*, for evaluating the copyright status of works created in the United States before 1977.[20] This resource is a comprehensive tool for better understanding the process for making public domain determinations, and any copyright review system would benefit from its guidance.

In the table below, we detail the primary research tools currently available for determining whether rights holders complied with US copyright formalities. Remember, these formalities applied during discrete periods of time and are no longer requirements for works being published today. Again, see *Copyright Term and the Public Domain in the United States* for a more detailed breakdown of the relevant time periods for these formalities.

December 31, 1949, renewal was required between December 31 of the year of the 27th anniversary of publication and December 31 of the year of the 28th anniversary of publication. See Sunstein Kann Murphy & Timbers, "Copyright Flowchart," accessed January 20, 2016, http://sunsteinlaw.com/practices/copyright-portfolio-development/copyright-pointers/copyright-flowchart/.

20 Menesha A. Mannapperuma, Brianna L. Schofield, Andrea K. Yankovsky, Lila Bailey, and Jennifer M. Urban. "Is It in the Public Domain?," last modified May 27, 2014, https://www.law.berkeley.edu/files/FINAL_PublicDomain_Handbook_FINAL%281%29.pdf.

US COPYRIGHT REVIEW—TABLE OF US COPYRIGHT FORMALITIES AND RESEARCH TOOLS

Below are the most effective tools and methods we have identified for copyright formality-related research:

US copyright formality	Review tool	Notes
Copyright renewal—Class A works (books)	Stanford Copyright Renewal Database[1]	The Stanford Copyright Renewal Database contains entries for all renewals of Class A works (books), published between 1923 and 1963. The Stanford database provides both simple and advanced search functions. The simple search function will let you search across all fields of Stanford's renewal record, while the advanced search focuses on specific fields, primarily "author" and "title." At minimum, we advise reviewers to perform searches on variations of the "first name + last name" of the author and only the last name of the author, along with full title and title keyword searches. Single searches are not advisable when they do not produce a result; reviewers should attempt multiple keyword variations before ending a search for a renewal record.

[1] Stanford University Libraries & Academic Information Resources. "Copyright Renewal Database," accessed January 20, 2016, http://collections.stanford.edu/copyrightrenewals/.

US copyright formality	Review tool	Notes
Copyright renewal—non–Class A works (periodicals, maps, photographs, etc.)	Catalog of Copyright Entries (CCE)[2]	The Catalog of Copyright Entries is a full listing of the registration and renewal records of the US Copyright Office, through 1978. Digital scans of the CCE, with searchable optical character recognition (OCR), are now available online. Because OCR can be of variable quality, your initial search should take advantage of keyword searches, but you should still browse the scan if the keyword searches yield no results.
Copyright renewal—non–Class A works (periodicals, maps, photographs, etc.)	US Copyright Office Catalog[3]	You will use the US Copyright Office Catalog to research the status of any non–Class A work first published on or after 1951. Please note that the Online Catalog is not a highly flexible search tool—do not expect a "first name + last name" search to be sufficient in most cases. As an example, go to the US Copyright Office Catalog. Select "name" and search "Kurt Vonnegut." Your search should result in approximately seven entries. Now search "Vonnegut Kurt." Your search will result in ~214 entries, many of which (far more than seven) are relevant to the author of *Slaughterhouse Five*. This is just one example of the inflexibility of the US Copyright Office Catalog—consequently, you should always try search variations when using this resource.

2 The Online Books Page. "Copyright Registration and Renewal Records," accessed January 20, 2016, http://onlinebooks.library.upenn.edu/cce/.

3 US Copyright Office. "Public Catalog," accessed January 20, 2016, http://cocatalog.loc.gov/cgi-bin/Pwebrecon.cgi?DB=local&PAGE=First.

US copyright formality	Review tool	Notes
Copyright notice	Reviewer should examine the work for evidence of a copyright notice.	Copyright notice review is based on the object itself. Page 26 of *Is It in the Public Domain?* contains a useful grid detailing the proper location of copyright notices for a range of material types. US Copyright Office's Circular 3, *Copyright Notice*, is also particularly helpful for better understanding the notice requirement.[4]

---

4 US Copyright Office. "Copyright Notice," last reviewed February 2013, accessed January 20, 2016, http://www.copyright.gov/circs/circ03.pdf.

Application: US State Government Documents (1923–77)

CRMS took the 1923–77 US copyright notice formality as the basis for a systematic copyright review of US state government documents. We consider the review of state government documents to be a valuable, large-scale, and low-risk area for review. There are over seventy thousand state government volumes currently in our candidate pool, making it a substantial body of work to review. We have also received numerous requests from scholars studying state documents and see this as rich territory for future scholarship.

Approximately 70 percent of the state government documents we reviewed did not bear a copyright notice. This implies that many state governments were relatively unconcerned about the copyright status of these works, as the absence of notice on these works injected them into the public domain.[21]

---

21 Note that US law required a formal copyright notice until 1989. However, from 1978 to 1989 there were exceptions to an absolute notice requirement. These included

LEGAL

17 U.S.C. § 104A: Copyright Restoration under the URAA

Copyright restoration means that many works first published outside the United States between 1923 and 1989 will be considered to be in copyright, even if the rights holders didn't comply with US copyright formalities of the time, including renewal and notice.

Copyright restoration is a wrinkle for copyright review systems that base their determinations on the renewal and notice requirements detailed above. The copyright in works first published outside of the United States may be restored, even when rights holders did not comply with US copyright formalities in existence at the time of publication. This can complicate copyright review, because your review system should account for both the non-US authorship of the work and the publication history of the work. These elements require additional time and research.

Restoration will *not* apply to works first published in the United States, nor to works published prior to 1923. We detail the key elements of

---

provisions, applicable after 1977, giving a rights holder five years after publication to cure omission of notice. See US Copyright Office, "Copyright Notice," last reviewed February 2013, accessed January 20, 2016, http://www.copyright.gov/circs/circ03.pdf. This is an area for individual institutional policy and process decisions—your team could choose to design a process to check for subsequent registration in that five-year window after publication without notice.

LEGAL

copyright restoration below, but you should consider reading the US Copyright Office's Circular 38b, *Copyright Restoration under the URAA* in order to understand the contours of restoration.

Per Circular 38b, a work is eligible for restoration provided *all* the following conditions are met:

1. At the time the work was created, at least one author (or rights holder in the case of a sound recording) must have been a national or domiciliary of an eligible source country. An eligible source country is a country, other than the United States, that is a member of the WTO, a member of the Berne Convention for the Protection of Literary and Artistic Works, or subject to a presidential proclamation restoring US copyright protection to works of that country on the basis of reciprocal treatment of the works of US nationals or domiciliaries.
2. The work is not in the public domain in the eligible source country through expiration of the term of protection.
3. The work is in the public domain in the United States because it did not comply with formalities imposed at any time by US law, lacked subject matter protection in the United States in the case of sound recordings fixed before February 15, 1972, or lacked national eligibility in the United States.

4. If published, the work must have been first published in an eligible country and not published in the United States during the 30-day period following its first publication in the eligible country.[22]

We have not identified robust tools to systematically address the fourth factor, the "simultaneous publication" (within thirty days) question. Instead, we primarily focus on the following questions: (1) is there non-US authorship in the work; (2) was the work in the public domain in its country of origin as of January 1, 1996;[23] and (3) was the work first published in the United States?

We used the Virtual International Authority File (VIAF) to help us identify non-US authors. We also used WorldCat to study the publication history of volumes where copyright restoration was likely.[24] Even with those tools, restoration is complicated territory and we do not have perfect answers for researching every factor. We do have some ideas, but they

---

22 We recommend anyone interested in copyright restoration begin by looking at US Copyright Circular 38b, from which the above text was drawn. US Copyright Office. "Copyright Restoration Under the URAA," last reviewed January 2013, accessed January 20, 2016, http://copyright.gov/circs/circ38b.pdf.

23 We consider 1996 to be the effective date of restoration for most countries—countries that were members of the WTO or the Berne Convention as of January 1, 1996. See 17 U.S.C. § 104A(h)(2)(A).

24 Online Computer Library Center. "WorldCat," accessed January 20, 2016, http://www.worldcat.org.

do not currently work at scale. Researchers wishing to perform additional research into the fourth factor, the "simultaneous publication" (within thirty days) question, may consider reviewing the publication date information discoverable in the Catalog of Copyright Entries and cross-referencing that information with publication notices in past volumes of trade publications.[25]

US Federal Government Documents (17 U.S.C. § 105)

Federal government documents are given a public domain determination. This is based on Section 105 of the Copyright Act, which disclaims US copyright protection for works of the US government: "Copyright protection under this title is not available for any work of the United States Government."[26]

US federal government documents have not been a focus of CRMS reviews, but we note the following observations in the *Compendium of US Copyright Office Practices* for any project that encounters questions related to the copyright status of federal government works:

---

25 We believe past trade publications, like *The Bookseller, A Newspaper of British and Foreign Literature,* may be useful for publication history research relevant to the simultaneous publication question.

26 17 U.S.C. § 105.

LEGAL

- Works prepared by officers or employees of the US Postal Service, the Corporation for Public Broadcasting, the Public Broadcasting Services, or National Public Radio are not considered works of the US government.
- Works prepared by officers or employees of the Smithsonian Institution are not considered works of the US government if the author-employee was paid from the Smithsonian trust fund.
- The US Secretary of Commerce may secure copyright for a limited term not to exceed five years in any standard reference data prepared or disseminated by the National Technical Information Service pursuant to 15 U.S.C. Chapter 23.[27]

In addition to the above carve-outs, we observed some confusion among librarians about what constitutes a federal government work. Typically, the answer to this question requires additional research into the agency and the agent that produced the work. Our guidepost for determining whether a work falls under Section 105 comes from the Section 101 definitions found in the Copyright Act: "A 'work of the United States Government' is a work prepared by an officer or employee of the United States Government as part of that person's official duties."[28]

---

27 US Copyright Office. "US Government Works," in Compendium of US Copyright Office Practices, § 313.6(C)(1) (3d ed. 2014) (internal citations omitted).

28 See 17 U.S.C. § 101 ("work of the United States Government").

CRMS-WORLD: BUILDING INTERNATIONAL COPYRIGHT EXPERTISE

International legal regimes tend to base the copyright term for a work on the life of its author plus a number of years. When we study the copyright laws of a non-US country, we try to identify the proper terms for the following types of authorship—works with (a) a known author, (b) known (multiple) authors, (c) unknown/anonymous author(s), (d) corporate authors, (e) government works, or (f) unpublished works.

If you are beginning to study the copyright law of a non-US country, you should reference the documents located at WIPO Lex.[29] This database aims to be an authoritative and up-to-date resource for international copyright law. Europeana's extensive public domain research documents, available online, are a rich, diverse resource for better understanding European copyright laws.[30] The most comprehensive and detailed treatise we have found regarding international copyright law is Geller and Nimmer's *International Copyright Law and Practice*.[31]

---

29 World Intellectual Property Organization. "WIPO Lex," accessed January 20, 2016, http://www.wipo.int/wipolex/en/.

30 Europeana. "Public Domain Calculator," accessed January 20, 2016, http://archive.outofcopyright.eu/index.html.

31 Paul Edward Geller and Melville B. Nimmer. *International Copyright Law and Practice* (Newark, NJ: Matthew Bender, 2009). This treatise provides extensive coverage of international copyright law and specific national chapters focused on the laws

LEGAL

It would be impossible to distill and do justice to the range of international legal regimes contained in *International Copyright Law and Practice*, but there are many features of international law that your project team should consider before embarking on projects involving copyright decisions that affect international works or implicate non-US jurisdictions.

Territoriality

Put simply, the copyright laws of any one country are not determinative for questions of copyright worldwide. Copyright law in other territories of the world is frequently different from the copyright laws we find in the United States. To cite one example, Canada features a copyright duration of life of the author plus fifty years,[32] which is twenty years less than the term of protection currently offered in the United States and many European countries. The consequences of this difference are very clear—in Canada, a work by an author who died in 1963 is in the public domain as of January 1, 2014, while a work by the same author may be protected by copyright in the UK until January 1, 2034.

---

of Argentina, Australia, Belgium, Brazil, Canada, China, France, Germany, Greece, Hong Kong, Hungary, India, Israel, Italy, Japan, Korea, the Netherlands, Poland, Spain, Sweden, Switzerland, the United Kingdom, and the United States.

32 Canadian Copyright Act. "Term of Copyright" (R.S.C., 1985, c. C-42, s. 6).

Additional coverage of the territoriality principle can be found in Goldstein and Hugenholtz's *International Copyright*[33] and Geller and Nimmer's *International Copyright Law and Practice*.[34] Your project team should be aware of territoriality and agree on a means for navigating it. CRMS-World determines the copyright term of works published in the UK based on UK copyright law and bases its copyright determinations for works published in Canada on Canadian copyright law.

National Treatment

National treatment means that, by operation of treaty, a foreign author will receive the same treatment as the nationals of the protecting country. In other words, if Spain and the UK have agreed to treat their nationals identically, Spain will grant copyright protection to UK authors for the same duration as Spanish authors. Likewise, the UK will grant copyright protection to Spanish authors for a term equal to UK authors.

As a consequence of national treatment, a Spanish court recently found that the works of G. K. Chesterton remained in copyright in Spain, despite

---

33 Paul Goldstein and Bernt Hugenholtz. *International Copyright: Principles, Law and Practice* (Oxford: Oxford University Press, 2013), 95.

34 Paul Edward Geller and Melville B. Nimmer. *International Copyright Law and Practice* (Newark, NJ: Matthew Bender, 2009).

their public domain status in the UK.[35] The Chesterton case is consistent with the *Phil Collins* case, a German decision in which the courts held that European Community nationals must be afforded national treatment with regard to copyright. Nationals of the UK, for example, would be afforded the same copyright duration in Spain as Spanish-born authors.[36] The German Federal Court of Justice, in a subsequent case, found that the works of Puccini, an Italian composer, were protected in Germany, despite the fact that Puccini died prior to the original 1958 European Economic Community treaty and that Puccini had a shorter term of protection in Italy.[37]

Special Cases

Your project planners should expect to encounter differences from one international copyright regime to the next. This baseline understanding will help to guide your planning, shape your project scoping and access decisions, and inform the ways you communicate with foreign rights holders.

---

35 Antonio Castán. "Chesterton Gains an Extra Decade through Spanish Transitional Provisions," last modified June 2, 2013, http://the1709blog.blogspot.com/2013/06/chesterton-gains-extra-decade-through.html.

36 Paul Edward Geller and Melville B. Nimmer. *International Copyright Law and Practice* (Newark, NJ: Matthew Bender, 2009). EU-26.

37 Paul Edward Geller and Melville B. Nimmer. *International Copyright Law and Practice* (Newark, NJ: Matthew Bender, 2009), EU-27.

LEGAL

Narrowing your scope is an important means of dealing with the complexity of international laws. Even with a narrow scope, you will need to attend to nuances and differences when developing review projects focused on international works. Below are a few examples of variations in the UK's copyright regime. These examples reflect some ways in which the international legal landscape does not always match up with a US-centric understanding of copyright law.

King James Bible

CRMS takes an admittedly conservative approach with regard to public domain determinations of versions of the Bible. Within the United States, we consider any version of the Bible published prior to 1923 to be in the public domain.

Outside the United States, we do not open versions of the Bible as public domain, based on UK law. This is largely due to the unique status of the King James Version, as noted on the Cambridge University Press website:

> Rights in The Authorized Version of the Bible (King James Version) in the United Kingdom are vested in the Crown and administered by the Crown's patentee, Cambridge University Press. The reproduction by any means of the text of the King James Version is permitted to a maximum of five hundred (500) verses for liturgical and noncommercial educational use, provided that the verses quoted neither amount to a complete book of the Bible nor represent

25 per cent or more of the total text of the work in which they are quoted.[38]

Though it was published in the seventeenth century and is out of copyright, control over the KJV Bible persists as a royal prerogative. While this may seem surprising, please remember the theme of this section: international legal regimes will not always match your understanding of US law.

Peter Pan

Like the King James Version of the Bible, we would consider the pre-1923 publications of *Peter Pan* to be in the public domain in the United States. However, we wouldn't apply that determination universally.[39] To understand the unique status of *Peter Pan*, again look at UK law:

> **Provisions for the benefit of the Hospital for Sick Children.**
>
> The provisions of Schedule 6 have effect for conferring on trustees for the benefit of the Hospital for Sick Children, Great Ormond Street, London, a right to a royalty in respect of the public performance,

---

38 Cambridge University Press. "Bibles, Rights and Permissions," accessed January 20, 2016, http://www.cambridge.org/index.php?cID=76100.

39 If a particular version of *Peter Pan* was published after 1922, that version may still be in copyright in the United States.

commercial publication or communication to the public of the play "Peter Pan" by Sir James Matthew Barrie, or of any adaptation of that work, notwithstanding that copyright in the work expired on 31st December 1987.[40]

Based on the standard copyright term in the UK, one would expect all J. M. Barrie's works to have entered the public domain in the UK. We only discover this variation by looking more closely at UK law and the legal commentary surrounding it.

---

40 UK Copyright, Designs and Patents Act, 1988, c. 48, s. 301. "Provisions for the benefit of the Hospital for Sick Children."

Crown Copyright

Figure 2 War Office seal, from the front pages of *A collection of minor wartime government publications,* https://babel.hathitrust.org/cgi/pt?id=uc1.b3039799;view=2up;seq=6;size=175

Crown copyright encompasses works produced by government agencies in Commonwealth countries. Like works of the US government, the copyright term for works covered by Crown copyright is not based on the life of the author of the work. Instead, copyright in a Crown work is typically held by the government for a period of years after publication.

For the three countries encompassed by our CRMS-World project, Crown copyright terms are as follows:

LEGAL

Australia: Year of publication + 50 years[41]
Canada: Year of publication + 50 years[42]
United Kingdom: Year of publication + 50 years[43]

To identify Crown copyright works, we instruct CRMS reviewers to look for indicia that a work from a Commonwealth country was prepared or published by or under the direction or control of Her Majesty or any government department. Frequently, Crown copyright works bear a "Crown Copyright Reserved" notice or carry some other indicator of government publication (such as the Royal Coat of Arms, above).

ADDITIONAL CONSIDERATIONS

CRMS seeks to address, as efficiently as possible, the copyright-related complexities inherent in many books. We typically handle complexity through policy decisions. As a consequence, our conservative determinations to keep works closed can sometimes be more practical than precise. In many gray-area cases, described more fully below, our more conservative positions are driven by a combination of risk tolerance and

---

41 Australian Copyright Act. "Duration of Crown copyright in original works," Copyright Act, 1968, s. 180(2).

42 Canadian Copyright Act. "Where Copyright Belongs to Her Majesty" (R.S.C., 1985, c. C-42, s. 12).

43 UK Copyright, Designs and Patents Act, 1988, c. 48, s. 163(3)(b).

LEGAL

a need for efficiency. The considerations below should be understood as part of the trade-off for making large-scale determinations. We encourage you to think about these issues with a critical eye; your review project may choose to approach the following issues differently.

Inserts

Inserts are third-party content incorporated into a work. When we talk about an insert, we may be referring to a range of materials—to cite a few examples, inserts include individual photographs, illustrations, and articles or chapters previously published in other works. The inserts issue greatly complicates copyright review. The issue is similar for both US-based copyright determinations and copyright determinations for international works. At its most fundamental, the insert issue is an information problem. We often can make a copyright determination for a given volume, but the copyright status of component parts may be impossible to determine or require extensive research.

For US books published 1923–63, a copyright determination for a book may be based on the presence or absence of a copyright renewal record in the Stanford Copyright Renewal Database. However, imagine that the book was not renewed but features fifty-three photographs, licensed from more than one photographer, for the purpose of providing illustrations for the book. We would treat those photographs as inserts and typically end the review with an und/nfi (undetermined/needs further investigation) determination, subject to future research.

LEGAL

Our inserts policy takes a conservative approach, one that has allowed us to move quickly through hundreds of thousands of reviews even though it may keep many works closed that may be properly in the public domain. While we do not review works with photograph inserts, we know that very few 1923–63 photographs were renewed. Inserts represent a very difficult information problem and our conservative stance is one approach to this problem.

Currently, the registration and renewal status of an individual photograph is not easy to determine. Registrations and renewals for individual photographs are findable in the Catalog of Copyright Entries. However, to our knowledge, no one has yet created a visual inventory of all renewed photographs that would allow a reviewer to cross reference a photograph contained in an otherwise public domain volume with the renewed photographs listed in the Catalog of Copyright Entries. Arguably, such an inventory could be created but, without some image search functionality, its usefulness is an open question.

There may be alternate ways to address this problem. We recognize that the concern for possible copyrights in a relatively small number of possible inserts results in a large number of closed (primarily und/nfi) works—over 46,000 volumes in CRMS-US alone. To illustrate the likely mismatch between our concern for inserts and the number of works likely to contain renewed, in-copyright insert material, consider the following additional data points:

LEGAL

- Very few photographs and illustrations published between 1923 and 1963 were actually renewed and would be still in copyright. In 1955, there were only 216 renewals for artwork and photographs.[44] In 1956, there were 256.[45]
- The renewal rate for these types of works was low; therefore, most are likely to be in the public domain.[46]

Based on the relatively small number of likely in-copyright inserts, others may choose to take a different approach.

---

[44] The Online Books Page. "Copyright Registrations for 1955," accessed January 20, 2016, http://onlinebooks.library.upenn.edu/cce/1955r.html.

[45] The Online Books Page. "Copyright Registrations for 1956," accessed January 20, 2016, http://onlinebooks.library.upenn.edu/cce/1956r.html.

[46] A photograph could still be considered "in copyright" if previously published in a work that was renewed.

The inserts problem adds a layer to the classic "orphan works problem." With orphan works, we either cannot identify a rights holder or no rights holder exists. With inserts, we cannot efficiently determine whether there is a rights holder and, if so, whether that rights holder continues to hold rights in the work or if the work has instead entered the public domain. This inquiry is complex for books but even more so when we consider serials, moving images, sound recordings and any other works featuring multiple rights holders.

Published versus Unpublished

The published/unpublished divide is an important distinction in US copyright law, with implications outside of the United States as well. A work *published* in the United States in 1960 may be in the public domain in the United States due to failure to comply with US copyright formalities from that time period, such as registration, renewal, and copyright notice. However, if the work was not published and remained unpublished after 2002, the work would be "in copyright" for the life of its author plus seventy years or 120 years from the date of its creation, depending on facts related to its authorship.[47] In the UK, to cite just one international example, many unpublished works will be in copyright until 2039 or later.[48]

---

47 Peter Hirtle. "Copyright Term and the Public Domain in the United States," last modified January 3, 2016, http://copyright.cornell.edu/resources/publicdomain.cfm.

48 The National Archive. "Copyright and Related Rights," last modified July 2013, http://www.nationalarchives.gov.uk/documents/information-management/copyright-related-rights.pdf ("literary, dramatic and musical works that were still unpublished when the current statute, the Copyright Designs and Patents Act 1988, came into force in 1989 will be in copyright until 2039 at the earliest—this is especially important in archives, where most material is classified as unpublished").

A key case articulating the published versus unpublished distinction in the United States is *Estate of Martin Luther King, Jr., Inc v. CBS, Inc.*[49] In that case, the court articulated the difference between publication and "non-divesting limited publication," which would not constitute publication for the purposes of US copyright law: "Only a general publication divested a common law copyright. A general publication occurred 'when a work was made available to members of the public at large without regard to their identity or what they intended to do with the work.' Conversely, a non-divesting limited publication was one that communicated the contents of a work to a select group and for a limited purpose, and without the right of diffusion, reproduction, distribution or sale. The issue before us is whether Dr. King's delivery of the speech was a general publication [internal citations omitted]."[50]

This distinction is important for archives. If a work was not published, which is the case for most archival collections, a copyright review will typically involve researching the death date of the author of the work. An unpublished letter, written in 1957 by an author who died in 2002, would be in copyright until 2073.[51] In contrast, a book published in 1957, and one that did not conform to copyright formalities of the time period, would be in the public domain in the United States today.

---

49 Estate of Martin Luther King, Jr., Inc. v. CBS, Inc., 194 F.3d 1211 (11th Cir. 1999).

50 *Id*. at 1214–15.

51 Peter Hirtle. "Copyright Term and the Public Domain in the United States," last modified January 3, 2016, http://copyright.cornell.edu/resources/publicdomain.cfm.

Application: Dissertations and Theses

Dissertations and theses are a rich resource housed in the collections of many libraries and archives throughout the United States. CRMS takes a conservative stance and does not currently review dissertations or theses because of the unsettled question of their publication status. Ultimately, your institution's position on whether a given dissertation or thesis volume was published or unpublished will drive your copyright determinations for these types of works.

If *published* between 1923 and 1989, a dissertation would have required a copyright notice; otherwise the work entered the public domain. A key question then becomes, was this dissertation in fact published? There is a spectrum of opinion on the publication status of dissertations—two noteworthy examples are Gail Clement and Melissa Levine's *Copyright and Publication Status of Pre-1978 Dissertations: A Content Analysis Approach*[52] and Peter Hirtle, Emily Hudson, and Andrew Kenyon's case study, "Dissertations, Theses, and Student Papers," found in *Copyright and Cultural Institutions*.[53]

---

52 Melissa Levine and Gail Clement. "Copyright and Publication Status of Pre-1978 Dissertations: A Content Analysis Approach," *Libraries and the Academy* 11, no. 3 (July 2011): 813–29, http://hdl.handle.net/2027.42/100239.

53 Peter Hirtle, Emily Hudson, and Andrew Kenyon. *Copyright and Cultural Institutions: Guidelines for Digitization for US Libraries, Archives, and Museums* (Ithaca, NY: Cornell University Library, 2009).

Clement and Levine's article identifies instances where dissertations are likely to be considered published, such as past publication in microfilm form through University Microfilms International (UMI).[54] Hirtle, Hudson, and Kenyon's study notes that the University of California, Berkeley, in its guidance on "Publishing your Dissertation," takes the following position: "The Attorney for the Regents has advised that shelving the dissertation or thesis voids the common law copyright."[55] In other words, Berkeley's view is that a dissertation shelved at Berkeley has met the requirements of publication.

At the very least, there is agreement that the publication status of a dissertation is a fact-specific inquiry. Any project that wishes to make public domain determinations for dissertations, based on publication and lack of notice (for dissertations published 1923–77) or failure to renew copyright (1923–63), will need to first take a position on the publication status of (1) dissertations that were placed on a library shelf and accessible to the general public and (2) dissertations that were distributed via microfilm through companies like UMI.

---

54 Melissa Levine and Gail Clement. "Copyright and Publication Status of Pre-1978 Dissertations: A Content Analysis Approach," *Libraries and the Academy* 11, no. 3 (July 2011): 823, http://hdl.handle.net/2027.42/100239.

55 Peter Hirtle, Emily Hudson, and Andrew Kenyon. *Copyright and Cultural Institutions: Guidelines for Digitization for US Libraries, Archives, and Museums* (Ithaca, NY: Cornell University Library, 2009), 232.

Some commentators feel that asking authors for permission to make dissertations available is the best route, regardless of the possibility that a given work may be in the public domain. In support of this approach, Kevin Smith has noted a recent case involving a student's dissertation, *Diversey v. Schmidly*, in which Andrew Diversey sued the University of New Mexico for copyright infringement.[56] Smith draws parallels between the Diversey case and retrospective digitization projects aimed at doctoral or masters' theses and dissertations. In doing so, he adds an additional factual question to those noted above: how do we know that the author has *authorized* publication of their dissertation?[57]

Libraries and archives serve a special societal function, and copyright favors uses that promote progress. Decision makers at institutions have a range of options for addressing the dissertation question at their respective institutions. They may (1) bear the costs, complexity, and potential dead ends of seeking permission from dissertation authors; (2) bear the cost of a public domain determination for these works, along with the possible cost of error (note that dissertations may be a particularly sensitive topic for authors); (3) articulate a strong fair use argument, consider bolstering it with a public domain determination process, and filter out all works that are likely "in copyright"; or (4) do nothing. In some

---

56 Diversey v. Schmidly, 738 F.3d 1196 (10th Cir. 2013).
57 Kevin Smith. "Copyright Roundup," last modified December 27, 2013, http://blogs.library.duke.edu/scholcomm/2013/12/27/copyright-roundup/.

cases, a combination of these approaches may be the most appropriate path forward.

For many institutions, taking no action would be considered poor stewardship of their collections. Others will adopt a "wait and see" approach to this question, learning from the successes and failures of other institutions. As institutions take a stance and work toward developing robust processes for larger community adoption, we anticipate there will be some lessons learned, and we hope that these are shared broadly.

While a retrospective copyright review project may often be the only means of opening older dissertations, this issue should serve as a catalyst for all academic institutions as they work with their current students to define and document rights to the student work. All institutions should take care to ensure that their right to distribute future dissertations is defined and well documented.

Additional Authors

For most pre-1978 books published in the United States, the publication date of the book is central to its copyright duration. Additional authors do not typically factor into the copyright duration calculation. A coauthored work published between 1923 and 1963 and not renewed will be in the public domain in the United States regardless of the life-spans of the coauthors.[58]

When working in any copyright regime that bases the duration of copyright on the life of the author plus some number of years, you must calculate the term using the death date of the last surviving author. This can result in some peculiar consequences for copyright review. For example, sometimes we are able to locate the death dates for three of four authors but the fourth is difficult or impossible to ascertain. This may be a modest contributor who died at a much later date than the lead authors, yet it can result in the entire work remaining closed.

Translations

The important thing to remember when working with translations is that there are at least two separate rights holders to consider when making a copyright determination. There will be a copyright in the underlying work, the source of the translation. There will also be a copyright in the translation itself. Therefore, your reviews should take into account both sets of rights.

To give a real-world example, suppose you are reviewing a modern translation of *Don Quixote*. The underlying work, written by Miguel de

---

58 That analysis may change if one of the authors of the work was not a US citizen or was domiciled outside of the United States—in those cases, restoration may apply.

Cervantes, entered the public domain long ago—the work was published in the early seventeenth century, and Cervantes died in 1616. If a recently deceased or still-living author, on the other hand, wrote a modern translation, then that translation may still be under copyright.

Multipart Monographs

Multipart monographs are works published over a span of years rather than a single year. This issue is of concern when the copyright in a particular set of volumes is based on publication date, rather than based on the life of the author plus some number of years.

An example of this issue would be a monograph first published in the United States in four parts on the following dates: 1922, 1925, 1927, and 1930. The first part would be in the public domain in the United States, based on its pre-1923 publication. The remaining volumes would be subject to registration, renewal, and notice requirements, so they may or may not be in the public domain. Further research would be required.

Similarly, a four-part monograph published in the United States in 1960, 1965, 1970, and 1979 would be subject to different sets of requirements. The 1960 part would have required copyright notice, registration, and renewal. The 1965 and 1970 volumes would have absolutely required notice, and the 1979 volume would have required notice or, in the absence of notice, registration within the subsequent five years.

LEGAL

Outside the United States, copyright determinations will be based on the death dates of the authors whose work is in the volume. When dealing with multipart monographs, you should watch for changing authorship over time.

OBSERVATIONS

The Importance of the und/nfi Category

One of the fundamental elements of the CRMS review process is the und/nfi (undetermined/needs further investigation) category, which is a decision-making outlet for reviewers who encounter works that present more complex issues of copyright. As an example, suppose you encounter a book first published in 1952 in the United States for which there is no copyright renewal record. Is that entire work in the public domain?[59] Does your answer to that question change if it contains illustrations or photographs?

A rights holder may have failed to renew copyright for a book published in 1952, effectively placing the book in the public domain, and yet component parts of the book may not be in the public domain. There may be a photo or illustration in the work that was individually registered

---

59 Failure to renew copyright in a work published in the United States between 1923 and 1963 places that work in the public domain for the purposes of US copyright law.

and renewed. As an example, Bessie Pease Gutmann's *Love's Blossom* was registered on April 20, 1927, and was renewed on March 4, 1955.[60] If this image were incorporated into a book published in 1952, and the author of that book failed to renew its copyright, that failure would not have thrust *Love's Blossom* into the public domain.

---

60 The renewal record for *Love's Blossom* can be found here: http://archive.org/stream/catalogofcopyrig39711libr#page/163/mode/1up.

Figure 3 Bessie Pease Gutmann's *Love's Blossom*. Image included here as an exercise of fair use.

CRMS is a production-oriented project, and our team did not have the time to research the copyright status of every individual image. When we encounter a work that includes credited content, we mark the work as und/nfi (due to inserts) and set it aside for determination at a future date.

This stance is a mix of risk assessment, copyright law, and pragmatism. Your project may consider alternatives that do not involve performing copyright determinations on each individual component part. However, we would caution against extensively and fully reviewing every insert; the process would quickly become bogged down. This is the value of the und/nfi category: it allows us to disregard excessively complex copyright objects and instead focus our energies on works that are much more likely to lead to a conclusive determination. At the same time, the und/nfi category is ripe with opportunity deferred.

Notice and Takedown

In *Copyright Risk Management: Principles and Strategies for Large-Scale Digitization Projects in Special Collections,* Kevin Smith notes that a good strategy for mitigating the risk associated with any digitization project is to have a takedown policy for materials that become subject to complaint.[61] The same may be said for a copyright review management project. While notice and takedown does not eliminate the possibility of a rights holder bringing suit, it does reduce the possibility and helps to avoid escalation of any issue that may arise. Taking a work down does not preclude the possibility of requesting permission to provide access to the work or studying the issue further and concluding that the work is properly in the public domain. A responsive takedown policy provides

---

61 Kevin Smith. "Copyright Risk Management: Principles and Strategies for Large-Scale Digitization Projects in Special Collections," *Research Library Issues*, no. 279 (June 2012): 17, http://publications.arl.org/rli279/17.

time to consider future actions without the additional stress of a pending complaint.[62]

Role of an Advisory Working Group: Oversight from Copyright Experts

To the extent that you are planning a long-term copyright review project and intend to review a broad range of material, you should consider forming a copyright advisory group for ongoing informal or formal consultation. If your project is small in scale, narrow in scope, and of limited duration, then an advisory working group may not be necessary. Given the complexity of copyright and the possibility that the legal landscape may evolve over the duration of any given copyright review project, it is worthwhile to have experts available to help with both predictable and unforeseen challenges or opportunities that may arise.[63]

An advisory working group will provide support when your project team faces difficult and legally complex questions. A mechanism for reaching out to experts and drawing on their expertise will benefit any large-scale

---

62 For a good example, see HathiTrust's takedown policy: HathiTrust. "Take-Down Policy," accessed January 20, 2016, https://www.hathitrust.org/take_down_policy.

63 As with many areas of law, it is best to be well informed and up-to-date regarding developments in copyright law. This is not a static area of law and an advisory group can help you stay apprised of any relevant developments.

LEGAL

project. CRMS had the advantage of being able to draw on the expertise of several copyright scholars and practitioners (see acknowledgments).

Your institution's legal counsel should either be directly involved with a proposed copyright review project or help identify experts to participate in advising your project team. The advisory group should include some participants from outside the institution who can provide fresh eyes for those times when your team needs an objective vantage point. If you are considering working with materials that implicate international legal regimes, consider identifying and collaborating with experts who have experience working with the laws of the relevant country.

We found that in-person meetings with our advisory group were an important way for us to check our processes and recalibrate practices as needed. While other forms of communication are often necessary, hashing out the details of a large-scale project benefits from in-person group discussion. Be prepared to hear a spectrum of opinions on any given topic and understand that you must ultimately decide which path makes sense for your institution. Your advisory group can provide good, meaningful feedback for your project, but issues related to legal liability, public scrutiny, and future relationships with rights holders ultimately begin and end with your own institution.

Partnership and Collaborative Work

Collaborative work offers many advantages. CRMS has benefitted greatly from the contributions of nineteen partner institutions and over

LEGAL

sixty copyright reviewers. In a given week, we collectively perform several thousand copyright reviews. In isolation, a single institution could not have accomplished the same outcome. By distributing the labor of copyright review, CRMS was able to accomplish over 300,000 copyright determinations for books published in the United States in less than six years' time, as well as over 172,000 determinations for books published in the UK, Canada, and Australia. This is a tribute to the individuals who contributed their time and energy to this process. It is also a testament to the power of distributed work.

While the above is a testimonial for cooperative partnership in your copyright review, keep in mind the legal and financial implications of working with a range of partners. Institutions engaging in copyright review projects cannot eliminate the risk of mistake—copyright is far too complex to ever design a completely error-proof system. This risk of error in copyright review projects should not be taken lightly, and the costs of mistakes can range from the institutional costs of remedying an error to the more profound consequences of a lawsuit.

CRMS worked to mitigate the risk of error by instituting double reviews, selecting expert reviewers who are fair but conservative in their adjudications, and managing our partner reviewers through training and regular feedback. However, as the number of reviewers increases, the time commitment of managing the activity also increases. Large-scale copyright review requires continued oversight and guidance. If you plan on performing this work on a large scale, be prepared to invest significant resources in its oversight.

PERMISSIONS AS AN ALTERNATIVE TO COPYRIGHT REVIEW

Copyright determinations may be unnecessary when rights holders are identifiable and willing to grant permission to make their works available online. HathiTrust has a standard permissions agreement that could be employed in coordination with rights holders controlling large numbers of works, see www.hathitrust.org/permissions_agreement.

As an example of this possibility, a future project may involve speaking with government organizations like the United Nations, to see if they'd be willing to grant permission to open relevant UN documents in HathiTrust. More broadly, permissions may be a good approach to providing access to large-scale collections when a single rights holder is readily identifiable.

LEGAL

Personnel

The size of the HathiTrust collection represented an incredible opportunity and an enormous task. Few institutions have the resources to accomplish over three hundred thousand copyright determinations in seven years. The willingness of nineteen institutions to work together made that achievement possible.

As CRMS grew in scale, we gained a better understanding of what remote collaboration could accomplish and what it required. Remote collaboration required significant investments in the development of tools and techniques to train and communicate with more than sixty reviewers in geographically diverse locations. Management of a large project required frequent communication with reviewers and their supervisors, maintenance of technical infrastructure, global access to the review interface, and consistent project documentation. This section offers insights on staffing, maintaining, and expanding a remote network of reviewers like those who made up CRMS.

SELECTING REVIEWERS

The skills suited to employment in other areas of the library are very similar to the skills needed to be a successful copyright reviewer. Your project should seek reviewers who demonstrate fine attention to detail, facility with a computer, and an ability to think critically. A willingness to ask questions and adapt are also very important reviewer traits. Because reviewers follow a defined decision tree, it is not necessary for them to be copyright "specialists" or to have more than a fairly basic knowledge of copyright law.

PERSONNEL

 Experience broadened our vision of who can be a successful copyright reviewer. We originally sought catalogers to participate in this activity because their data collection skills and disciplined process orientation transferred well to the copyright review process. However, while these skills are valuable, they are certainly not exclusive to degreed information professionals. While we initially preferred trained librarians, we had excellent experience with graduate student reviewers and library assistants with proper oversight.

It is important to select reviewers with pattern recognition and critical thinking skills. The realm of the possible in monographic publishing is immense and varied. Often a single phrase or caption in a volume can affect a decision, and that kind of examination requires thorough attention to detail and an ability to think critically. Training will not be able to cover every eventuality. However, if done correctly, it will enable reviewers to understand why decisions are made and how they can apply their knowledge in new situations.

We do not enforce a production mind-set on our reviewers, but some reviewers exhibit this tendency and execute a high number of determinations. Others take their time on detailed searches for an elusive author death date. Either characteristic could be more or less attractive based on the desired outcomes of your project. In our experience, the accuracy of reviews is relatively consistent across reviewers regardless of individual pace and work styles. If you ask your reviewers to focus on high production numbers, you should anticipate that a greater percentage of reviews will be indeterminate, as reviewers will set more complex volumes aside. For projects with a focus on higher determinacy, reviewers will take more time or require more specialized resources.

PERSONNEL

ENVIRONMENTAL FACTORS INFLUENCING REVIEWERS

Environment plays a profound role in this work. Before jumping to conclusions about a reviewer's suitability, first investigate any external factors that may be having a negative impact on the reviewer's performance. Removing or reducing environmental distractions is important. Giving a reviewer a quiet space in which to work in a focused manner, free from distractions and competing responsibilities, will often improve the reviewer's productivity and accuracy. In other words, copyright review should not be done during a reference desk shift.

Scans are often very detailed, so proper equipment is an equally important consideration. On occasion, we found that an apparent problem with a reviewer could often be resolved by upgrading the reviewer's equipment. Small screens that cannot display an entire page run the risk of obscuring information important to a copyright determination. A widescreen monitor will provide enough real estate to view works at sufficient resolution for a thorough review.

TIME COMMITMENTS

The first step in bringing new reviewers onto the CRMS project is securing a formal and documented commitment from the partner institution. A specific time commitment for each reviewer is essential, given the substantial resources the CRMS management team expends in training them. The time commitment for a reviewer must be reasonable and achievable, and it should be settled prior to the commencement of training. After several years of observations and discussions with CRMS partners, we can offer recommendations for reviewer time commitments.

Minimum Time Commitments As with any skill that requires practice to attain proficiency, copyright review requires a minimum weekly time commitment for review skills to remain at their sharpest. One of our first observations in CRMS-World was that a majority of reviewers who had a time commitment of 5 percent FTE (a full time equivalent of two hours a week) either stopped performing reviews altogether or voluntarily increased their time. From this we concluded that working two hours per week on copyright review is not a sustainable model for maintaining engagement.

Maximum Time Commitments We noticed a decline in productivity for those reviewers who had time commitments at 33 percent to 50 percent FTE (thirteen to twenty hours per week). Many of these reviewers were not reaching the numbers we would have expected given the productivity of reviewers working at lower time commitments. We sampled average productivity biannually during the first two years and found that the decline in productivity seemed to affect those at 33 percent FTE or greater time commitments.

Further Consideration Discussions with our partners brought to light information that might explain these observations. Some of the reviewers assigned to higher time commitments also held managerial positions within their library. Their concurrent job priorities competed for time with CRMS. To compound the issue, the copyright review process itself is very repetitive and tedious when performed at length. Personally

PERSONNEL

we have found that twenty hours a week or longer performing copyright review is unsustainable in the long term. We would caution project planners against having unrealistic expectations of reviewers.

Our current position is that a time commitment between 15–25 percent FTE (six to ten hours per week) is ideal. Reviewers will have sufficient time to retain skills without the risk of overload. We recognize that, ultimately, your project team will have to allocate human resources based on the priorities of your institution. We accommodated time commitments outside of our recommended range; however, it is best to understand the staffing implications when discussing project expectations with your partners.

SECURITY AND AUTHORIZING REVIEWERS FOR ACCESS

A fundamental requirement of the CRMS copyright review process is access to potentially in-copyright digital scans. We gained access to scans by partnering with HathiTrust, which manages the security and authorization mechanism. Pulling physical books from the library shelves is a viable choice for copyright review, but not for a project at this scale.

HathiTrust and the University of Michigan Library impose access restrictions to protect the system infrastructure and the copyrighted material under review. This made it unnecessary for the CRMS project team to develop an access control system of our own. Access restrictions are expensive and challenging to develop, so the opportunity to comply with HathiTrust's established and robust system was a significant advantage for CRMS.

For each individual CRMS reviewer, the CRMS project manager works with HathiTrust to authorize access to digital scans. Authorization is limited by purpose, location, and time. Reviewers may only use their access for the purposes of copyright review, and the digital scans can only be accessed from their designated IP address. After a set time (usually six months), the reviewer must sign a new "Statement for Access" form in order to renew the reviewer's access.

In order to receive authorized access and perform copyright reviews, all reviewers must have the following:

- A workstation in a secure staff area, not a public terminal
- An exclusive and static IP address
- A current browser (Firefox, Chrome, or Opera; preferably not Internet Explorer)
- Approval from a library dean or equivalent at the partnering institution
- A completed HathiTrust "Statement for Access Form"
- Approval from HathiTrust executive director
- A workstation registered with HathiTrust via a onetime access key
- Authorization from U-M systems to access the CRMS server

PERSONNEL

TRAINING

It is our observation that a centrally run training program works better than a distributed "train the trainer" approach. If you intend to have a large group of participants on your project, your team should include someone who is familiar with instructional design and has teaching experience. This person should also keep up their skills by participating in copyright review regularly. A supervisor who knows theory but does not regularly perform copyright review will not have the practical experience necessary to reliably teach the research process. A good and responsive trainer must also be prepared to answer questions and manage personal communication, serving as a primary contact for the reviewers throughout the project.

Once a staff member has been designated and both parties agree that her time commitment is reasonable and achievable, then she needs to proceed through a training process. We budget approximately ten hours of managerial time per person for training. The length of time a staff member needs to complete training depends on her ability and the amount of time she can devote each day to it. It can take between three weeks to three months for a new reviewer to complete training, averaging at around a month and a half.

We have experimented with both one-on-one tutoring and group training methods. There are pros and cons to each approach. One-on-one tutoring does not require a time investment in the creation of online learning objects such as videos and tests, and trainers can schedule individual sessions to give demonstrations and comments via screen sharing. Essentially private tutoring, this method adds an element of personal accountability and can more quickly help confirm concept mastery. It is also the most time-intensive method for the training team and does not scale up well. No more than three trainees assigned per tutor is a good rule to follow with this method. We employ it when there are only a few people who must be trained quickly.

We expected a group class method to make training move more quickly while also saving staff time. With it we were able to scale up in a way that was not possible with individual tutoring. Hosting group classes also confined training to discrete and scheduled cycles, giving the management team a break from constant activity. We did this by creating video tutorials and online testing modules that were part of a standardized educational plan. This was intended to give all trainees as similar an experience as possible, minimizing gaps in topic coverage. We reused the course videos and documents for several subsequent cycles, but after two years, the majority were in need of updating. Overall, group training does not significantly reduce the amount of time needed from the management team but shifts it to other activities.

During the training period, the management team will engage in the following tasks:

- Leading videoconferences to introduce the project and provide a basic foundation
- Grading and providing feedback on comprehension tests

PERSONNEL

- Answering daily questions
- Adjudicating practice reviews
- Communicating weekly progress to supervisors
- Providing individual tutoring as needed
- Troubleshooting system access problems

Group training does enable a higher volume of people to be trained but results in much longer training periods. Factors that may increase the length of training time include supervisors not allotting the trainee enough time to do the work, access problems in the computing environment, and environmental factors like too small a monitor. A group training class of about fifteen trainees can typically require two months or more.

DISTANCE LEARNING

Early training of CRMS reviewers happened on site at the University of Michigan. This was logistically difficult, with high costs for travel and hosting. As our institutional partners and reviewers have increased in number over time, in-person training has become more of a barrier to flexibility in making necessary personnel changes. Personnel changes were needed as staff retired or were transferred to other jobs. Robust distance learning options helped the project adapt to midstream staffing changes.

One of the fundamental elements of the CRMS grant was to study possible methods for sharing large-scale copyright review among institutions. Our CRMS grant explicitly pointed to online training as a vehicle for extending the work more broadly: "Online Training: We will develop and implement a web-based online training course to teach qualified librarians and similar professionals to be reviewers so they may make copyright determinations. This process will be refined and documented in the pre-grant period, reviewed, and validated by the Advisory Working Group. This will allow us to scale up the number of reviewers over the course of the grant."[64]

Distance learning fulfilled its promise, and we now rely exclusively on remote training for bringing new reviewers into the system. We have explored a number of remote training tools, which we discuss in the following sections.

SANDBOX

In order to give trainees a chance to practice, we created a static "sandbox" instance of the review interface. The sandbox is a clone of the production interface but totally separate, so any mistake a trainee makes has absolutely no impact on daily CRMS production. This offers new reviewers the opportunity to become accustomed to the tools they will

---

64 CRMS-World, IMLS National Leadership Grant LG-05-11-0150-11.

be using. Hands-on practice in the sandbox makes it easier to visualize and internalize the decision-making steps.

The sandbox is populated with recently validated reviews pulled from production. A new trainee needs only to complete the second review of the pair and their work can be checked against the first. This takes advantage of work produced by experienced reviewers and allows us to simulate pairing new recruits with veteran reviewers. In a relatively short period of time, we can gauge how quickly new reviewers are learning CRMS practices and also better understand any areas of confusion.

The sandbox system requires secure authorization, which may take a few days to complete. While waiting for authorization, trainees are asked to study CRMS documentation and demonstrate a basic understanding of the process. We administer two short tests of multiple-choice and short-answer questions to confirm their mastery of the process. Once they pass, trainees are free to work independently within the sandbox.

OTHER TRAINING TOOLS

A number of additional tools have proven useful for training reviewers. Most are general library-supported products or more affordable options.

- *Qualtrics.* Used to create "open-book" tests in which the answers are validated and a report is automatically e-mailed to the instructors via trigger e-mail. Qualtrics provides results in a PDF format

PERSONNEL

for trainees to refer to, with instructor commentary on missed answers. (See appendices for examples of two Qualtrics tests used in the project.)

- *Adobe Acrobat Professional.* Used to add instructor comments onto PDF format survey/test results.
- *Skype or BlueJeans videoconferencing.* Used to connect with trainees in one-on-one sessions. Screen-sharing features allow trainees to go through several reviews while the instructor prompts them with additional questions and commentary. For a time, Skype did away with its screen-sharing ability unless you paid for a premium subscription, and we also had trouble installing the client on computers at some institutions. On the whole, BlueJeans performed better with diverse computing environments, but the interface was moderately less intuitive and required more explanation for some trainees.
- *Headset microphones.* Used to allow hands-free videoconference screen sharing while demonstrating reviews. Generally trainees can borrow a headset microphone for the few days that they require it.
- *MediaWiki.* Used to provide a password-protected wiki site to document common questions and reviewer scenarios. This is a good knowledge-sharing tool and allows reviewers to seek answers to commonly asked questions.
- *Camtasia Studio.* Used to create screen capture videos with voice-over and captioning to demonstrate basic steps and actions taken within the interface. The videos are stored online and can be used to demonstrate features of the project to outside observers. This is

immensely helpful for demonstrating features of the CRMS system and interface.
- *Flowcharting software.* Used to diagram a workflow and create CRMS decision trees. Free online programs did not permit us to create charts that could be easily edited; Microsoft Word proved to be a flexible, lightweight, readily available alternative that allowed us to easily update workflow documentation as needed.
- *MediaGallery (U-M Library's video content management system).* Used to host screencast videos in a location where anyone with the link can gain access and view them. Online sites such as Screencast.com could work as well, but we ran into bandwidth limits using the free service. This was not sustainable, as videos could not be viewed until the bandwidth was reset in the next month.

READINESS FOR PRODUCTION

Trainees were required to complete a minimum of one hundred practice reviews with over a 92 percent accuracy rate before they were approved for production. This desired accuracy rate confirmed a reviewer's ability to follow CRMS processes. If trainees did not meet this standard, we assessed their invalidated reviews and worked with them to improve their understanding of the CRMS process.

REVIEWER COMMUNICATION

There are a number of ways in which we communicate directly with reviewers rather than through their supervisor. These communications are intended to motivate, build community, announce policy changes, and share data about individual and group progress.

Some of the communication methods we tested were less useful than anticipated. One was the chat reference tool Zoho that we linked to the sandbox interface. It was intended to provide real time Q&A with the experts for a trainee in the process of doing a copyright review. We stopped using Zoho chat after learning that it was difficult to maintain staffing with only three people who could provide reference. Also, the trainees preferred getting an answer by e-mail so they could archive the response.

Likewise, we explored the notion of displaying a personal "progress toward goal" bar. This would be able to track the number of minutes reviewers spent in the system and display a thermometer chart of their monthly progress. However, this was not an accurate metric for the time actually spent doing work on reviews. In the end, we decided not to implement this feedback tool because the inaccuracy could be demotivational.

Quite a few of the methods we tested have been effective, and we continued to use and refine them throughout the course of the project:

PERSONNEL

- *All-reviewer e-mail group.* Any reviewer can post a question, share an interesting item, or report technical troubles. The way reviewers use this group has changed over time, both with their comfort level in doing reviews and as the number of people on the list has grown. At the start of the project, it was highly useful to help calibrate decision making during reviews. Toward the end of the project, it became primarily an arena for notifying others of access and outage problems.
- *Trainee-only e-mail group.* A closed group available only to new people during a training period. This provides a semiprivate space to ask questions.
- *All-reviewer conference calls.* Scheduled twice a year via Adobe-Connect. We use the conference calls to update reviewers on CRMS practices, share helpful tips, introduce resources that will make review work easier, and provide general progress updates. The calls help everyone feel connected to the project as a whole and its goals.
- *Weekly automated data e-mail.* A lightweight stats report sent Wednesday mornings to all reviewers, giving a snapshot of how each institution did the previous week. It is a friendly motivator and a convenient reminder to contribute time each week to the project.
- *Trigger e-mail following seven days of inactivity.* An e-mail triggered on an individual basis when a reviewer has not been in the system for seven days. It reminds inactive reviewers to contact their supervisor or us if their availability has changed.

- *Personal stats display.* A personal tally page within the interface that updates daily to display personal number of reviews accomplished, minutes worked, and validation statistics. Some reviewers track this information more closely than others and are motivated by it.
- *Historical reviews.* An interface for searching all determinations made during the project. Searchable by user and verdict so reviewers may check and learn from their reviews or the reviews of others.

BENCHMARKING AND ONGOING REVIEWER MANAGEMENT

In order to assess and manage reviewer time commitments, you should have a system for benchmarking productivity that helps to set expectations while recognizing the complexity of copyright law. This is more art than science, and we are attentive to the fact that some reviewers take longer to reach a determination and some have time-intensive research skills that others do not. From our perspective, reviewers with a diversity of research skills, speed, and persistence can complement each other to great effect. With that said, we recommend establishing reasonable baseline expectations, along with mechanisms for holding reviewers to those standards.

It is difficult to set performance goals without an idea of how many can reasonably be done within a time period. At the beginning of a project, work with your reviewers to study the time required to perform a set number of reviews. Identify the percentage of public domain,

PERSONNEL

in-copyright, and undetermined volumes in your sample and evaluate whether adjusting productivity benchmarks would improve the determinacy outcomes. From that sample, set your benchmarks for productivity. Build flexibility and room to breathe into your standards and be sure to assess your benchmarks as the project evolves.

We would encourage you to consider both speed and determinacy when setting standards for your project. A high-determinacy project will likely require more time per volume; a high-production project may by necessity set more volumes aside as undetermined.

EXPERTS

As part of the CRMS review process, two different reviewers look at each candidate volume independently. If their results match, their shared judgment is accepted. If their results do not match, then there is a conflict, and an expert evaluates both independent reviews and adjudicates between them. An expert in CRMS is a reviewer with substantial review work experience who has demonstrated a high level of knowledge of CRMS processes. After receiving additional training, experts are qualified to examine and adjudicate mismatches in the copyright determinations of their fellow reviewers.

Having an appropriate number of experts is necessary to avoid a bottleneck in the workflow. Roughly 30 percent of reviews require an expert adjudication. We have found that an individual expert reviewer can look at approximately 200 conflicts a day. A system of similar scale to CRMS-World, which generates about 130 new conflicts per day, would ideally involve four trained experts. This number provides a margin of safety in the event of staffing changes and helps distribute the workload.

SUPERVISOR COMMUNICATION

Clear and regular communication with partner institution supervisors is the key to helping CRMS reviewers meet their time commitments, as copyright review work often competes for time and attention with other high-priority institution-specific work. When communicating with supervisors, we work to ensure that CRMS reviewers can commit the time and attention necessary and are not overwhelmed by competing priorities. When committing people to new work, supervisors must consider what other duties will need to be reduced.

We saw some areas where additional materials could help facilitate communication with supervisors, including the following:

- A CRMS reviewer job description that can be placed in a personnel file and used to discuss the work with supervisors who are unfamiliar and may otherwise see the work as "extra" rather than part of regular duties
- An "external administrator" role that allows a supervisor to view personal statistics of reviewers at that institution

PERSONNEL

- A weekly inactivity report that is used to discuss personnel changes and absences with supervisors

CRMS, as a cross institutional collaboration, has benefitted from thoughtful development of our modes of communication. The swift increase in the project scale made informal communication methods less effective with a large group. Communication requires time and human resources, but it is vital to the health of a large-scale project.

COST-SHARE REPORTS

Cost-share partnerships have been a part of CRMS since the start of the second National Leadership Grant from the Institute for Museum and Library Services (IMLS) in 2011. Cost-share partner institutions must report their contribution toward the overall grant match required by IMLS. Tracking partners' progress and financial reporting is a significant administrative undertaking.

It was tempting for supervisors and reviewers to think of contributions to the project solely in terms of the number of hours spent working with the interface. However, the cost-share commitments were expressed in dollar amounts, so the reviewers' salaries were the critical factor when tracking fulfillment. This could make replacing a departing reviewer more complicated if the incoming reviewer made a different wage because the new arrival would have to devote a different number of hours to the project in order to match a predecessor's contribution.

Cost-share management, therefore, also depended on education and regular updates for supervisors at the partner institutions. If a partner began falling behind on a commitment, the earlier we notified them the easier it was for them to make up the difference.

Verification

It is important to build checks on your processes and assumptions so you can be confident your system is working as intended and address any unforeseen issues when necessary. Internally, we have added forms of verification directly into our review process. In-house verification is one method, but working with an independent, third party is a valuable additional means of verification. Consider engaging third-party examinations to better evaluate the accuracy of your results. Methods of verification should focus on two areas: results and process.

DOUBLE REVIEW

We are committed to the double-review process, particularly for copyright review projects operating at a large scale. This process requires two separate, independent reviewers to agree on the rights status of a work. If the two reviews do not agree, a third, expert reviewer adjudicates the two reviews and decides the most appropriate determination for the volume.

The double review is a form of verification that provides CRMS with a daily check on our determinations. We have a high degree of confidence in our results because each review is performed at least twice and conflicting reviews receive additional attention from an expert reviewer. This does not protect against any underlying flaws in our methods, but it helps prevent human error from having large-scale consequences.

VERIFICATION

The double-review process creates an additional cost in time and labor. We could approximately double our reviews with the same amount of reviewer labor if we migrated our process to a single review system, but we would lose the immediate check on our results and be concerned that errors might more easily creep into our determinations.

COPYRIGHT REVIEW VERIFICATION

This verification process contemplates a future where reviewers at HathiTrust partners independently perform large-scale copyright review of volumes in the HathiTrust corpus. For example, the University of Wisconsin may wish to contribute copyright determinations for ten thousand works published in Ireland prior to 1945. In order for those reviews to be ingested into HathiTrust, they must be acceptable to HathiTrust's legal counsel (currently the Office of General Counsel at the University of Michigan). A verification process can give counsel a degree of confidence in the reliability of a project's results.

There are two stages to the verification process, outlined in the next section.

Preproject Verification

Preproject verification would include a review of all project documentation for the proposed project, feedback on project design if necessary, and a recommendation to approve or deny approval of the project

VERIFICATION

based on the legal assumptions and project planning documents submitted for review. Legal expertise is essential at this stage, but a focus on process is equally important.

The verification process should focus on any flawed legal assumptions in the project, problematic project design choices, or any other errors that could undermine project results. If errors are identified in the preproject stage, applicants should be given time to address them and submit revised project documentation.

Stage 1: Process Verification

The following questions are relevant to the design of the review project and can serve as a foundation for your inquiry.

Legal
1. What has the project team identified as relevant copyright durations for the following types of works?
   a. Known author
   b. Known (multiple) authors
   c. Unknown/anonymous author(s)
   d. Works published posthumously
   e. Corporate authors
   f. Government works
   g. Unpublished works
2. Does the project account for the presence of third-party materials in volumes being reviewed? Document the reason or justification

for accounting for—or choosing not to account for—third-party materials. This will affect decision making and the review process.
3. Are copyright duration calculations appropriately cited and verified?
4. What legal resources were used in developing the project plan and decision trees? Does the project's legal analysis and workflow correspond appropriately with the legal resources cited?
5. Is the review interface code a reliable translation of the project's legal analysis? (Note that ideally a second programmer would be available to confirm the accuracy of the code.)

Procedural
1. Foreign language expertise may be necessary to collect facts relevant to a copyright determination. Do reviewers for the project have adequate language expertise to perform the reviews? Is any other expertise required by this project?
2. Is a double review part of the project plan? If no, what is the justification for a single review?
3. Has the project team developed a decision tree to guide copyright determinations? Is it practical? Is it legally accurate?
4. What changes, if any, are recommended before this project moves forward?
5. Does the team recommend that the project commence reviews, based on the planning documents submitted?

Stage 2: Results Verification

The second stage should be a third-party verification of randomly sampled results, drawn from the project's volumes reviewed to date. This independent review should be designed to verify that the copyright determinations produced by the project are accurate and consistent with the previously approved project documentation. This review should be performed at an early stage in the project so that any errors can be identified and the review process can be modified when necessary.

All identified errors must be corrected, as well as any consistent patterns of error that are discovered through the verification. For example, if a particular author was misidentified, all volumes tied to that author should be re-reviewed. If narrow, easily fixed errors account for the error rate, no new check will be required after these errors have been corrected.

If the errors represent patterns that might have a broad impact on the rest of the candidate pool, the project will need to conduct a re-review of some percentage of the candidate pool. The re-review should focus on the source of the errors, whether due to human error, flawed legal assumptions, application code, or problems related to the review process. The re-review should be performed as narrowly as is reasonable, given the error, and at its conclusion, a new random verification sample should be generated.

VERIFICATION

 CRMS commissioned the US Copyright Office to check a small sample of CRMS-US reviews at an early stage of the project. Similarly, CRMS worked with Limited Times, LLC to employ their Durationator, a tool for assessing public domain status. The results from both checks were consistent with our findings. The challenge of using these resources is a practical problem at the heart of copyright determination work: you need to have a significant amount of information to use these resources effectively. The verification can only be as valid and useful as the metadata that you provide. This information gap is at the center of the notion of copyright as a design problem.

Funding

Large-scale copyright review requires sustained funding over a long period of time, and your institution must be prepared to make a substantial financial commitment to this activity. Start-up costs for copyright review can be high, as they include legal research, developing review tools, building management infrastructure, and training reviewers. The core of CRMS's success—over 450,000 volumes determined—was made possible by continued financial commitment beyond the start-up phase of the project.

While CRMS has been the beneficiary of generous and sustained funding, we would also like to note several elements specific to cost-share funding that your project team should consider when developing your project and considering its administration.

COST-SHARE REPORTING

Many grants require the applicant to provide matching funds for the grant activities. A 1:1 match is a typical arrangement. Cost-share occurs when this match is spread out across multiple institutions, through the commitment of personnel time or other financial contributions.

One significant administrative element of multi-institution cost-share collaboration is documentation. You must carefully document the cost-share of partner institutions, monitor their progress toward the cost-share commitment, and work with institutions if and when they are not meeting their cost-share obligations. Given the contractual nature of cost-share, it is very important that all partner institutions meet their commitments.

As the number of institutions formally committed to a project grows, the administrative workload for cost-share will also grow. While the payoff in multi-institution collaboration is worth the additional administrative workload, it is a substantial administrative workload, can be very time consuming, and must be considered as part of your project planning.

CHALLENGES TO FLEXIBILITY

The second significant issue to consider—also tied to cost-share—is that staff positions at institutions change over time, and the set financial commitment represented by a cost-share commitment can be a challenge to the flexibility of the project.

Although a cost-share commitment is represented as a percentage of staff time, individual compensation rates often differ. This can be a challenge to staffing when an employee earning a higher rate retires or is replaced by an employee earning a lower rate.

As an example, if University A has made a commitment of 25 percent of a given employee's time to your project, and that commitment equates to a $15,000 per year cost-share commitment, what happens if that employee retires? University A is still committed to a $15,000 per year cost-share with the project. But if University A tries to substitute a graduate student working ten hours a week at $15 per hour, that substitution would only represent a $7,800 commitment per year. University A would need to make up the difference of $7,200 each year.

This issue requires a clear understanding of the metrics used to manage and document a project. It is advisable to consider this at an early stage of planning. Closely collaborating with supervisors, setting expectations, and giving frequent progress updates will help cost-share partners meet their commitments.

We have seen the successes achievable when a large number of reviewers are focused on a shared goal. We are sincerely amazed by the work CRMS reviewers have completed over the course of the project. We also recognize the value of very specific, narrow projects undertaken on a smaller scale.

If your project is narrower in scope or does not require a cost-share model, we recommend seeking grants that will not incur the administrative costs associated with managing time and cost commitments from multiple outside institutions.

INSTITUTIONAL FUNDING

Long-term institutional funding of copyright review provides a number of advantages in terms of project strength and flexibility. The institution's financial commitment creates a stable environment for project management, training, and maintenance. Flux in the project team will threaten the continuity and expertise of the project. A lengthy break in funding would demand a substantial investment of resources and time to restart the activity.

If systematic copyright review is to continue as a long-term priority for your institution, we believe the institution must eventually fund the work directly, rather than primarily relying on grant funding resources.

Technical

ABOUT THIS TECHNICAL SECTION

The success of CRMS lies in its review process and the technical infrastructure that supports it. The CRMS interface presents a scanned image of a work in HathiTrust; the reviewer makes a copyright determination on the volume using the interface and the research tools the interface makes available (Stanford Copyright Renewal Database, the Virtual International Authority File [VIAF], etc.). The system stores a record of that determination, and, when appropriate, the system then exports the determination to the HathiTrust Rights Database. The system also includes methods for verifying reviews and determinations.

Access to scanned images of works in HathiTrust is essential to CRMS, as it would be to any copyright determination project at a comparable scale. This technical section therefore presumes that your project will be working with digital scans. Physical volumes are time-consuming and inefficient to manage by comparison.

Background

Copyright determination at the University of Michigan Library did not begin with CRMS. By the time the first version of CRMS went online in 2009, the staff of the Electronic Resource Access Unit had already conducted rights research on over 55,000 volumes in HathiTrust. This would have been an impressive accomplishment in and of itself, but the reviewers were working "manually" with only Excel spreadsheets and cumbersome automation. Their rights determinations were exported to the HathiTrust Rights Database monthly.

The first IMLS grant allowed the CRMS project team to streamline the rights research process by consolidating everything required for a copyright determination into one online interface. Reviewers had easy access to the scanned volume, several information resources to assist in making a determination, and a searchable database of all past rights determinations. The design of the system ensured the reliability of the determinations by requiring at least two reviewers for each volume and introduced a "conflicts" interface for expert reviewers who could adjudicate whenever reviewers disagreed. An automated processing script exported determinations to the HathiTrust Rights Database each night. After seven months of development, the first version of CRMS-US went live in July 2009.[65] The development of a training site for CRMS reviewers in May 2010 was also an opportunity to add functionality to allow system access for reviewers from Indiana University, the University of Minnesota, and the University of Wisconsin, all of whom began contributing work the following July.

The second IMLS grant allowed the CRMS project team to adapt the CRMS interface for rights research on non-US works. Development of the CRMS-World interface required five months. Testing in late April

---

65 At the time, the system was known only as CRMS. The project team later gave it the name "CRMS-US" to distinguish it from the "CRMS-World" interface.

TECHNICAL

2012 had the new version ready in time for the first CRMS-World training summit in early May. More rounds of testing and development followed that summer. A large part of the development effort for CRMS-World was concerned with migrating nonshared information from the source HTML and Perl code into the database and configuration files and making it possible for these to be extracted and used at runtime. An example of this is the list of information sources made available to reviewers for copyright research: CRMS-US uses the Stanford Copyright Renewal Database, whereas CRMS-World includes a number of other tools such as VIAF. The goal was to have everything differentiating the two systems be part of the database or configuration file, avoiding hardcoding to the greatest extent possible.

The development of CRMS-World had the advantage of starting from what was by then a mature CRMS codebase. The system could detect which "mode" (US or World) to run in and dynamically choose the interface and backend logic components that were appropriate for each reviewer. This shared codebase reduced maintenance costs because a tool written for one mode would work largely unchanged in the other. In a very real sense, CRMS-US and CRMS-World were one system that "came in two flavors," one formality-based and the other author-based.[66]

---

66 For more information on the distinction between copyright formalities and copyright determinations based on the life of an author, see the legal section.

TECHNICAL

A GLOSSARY OF TERMS USEFUL FOR COPYRIGHT DETERMINATION

Like any complex project, CRMS has acquired its own vocabulary. Here, we provide definitions to our terms in four main categories:

1. Objects being reviewed
2. User roles
3. Interface/system
4. Rights determination

This glossary can also be found in the appendices, with terms listed in alphabetical order.

1. Objects Being Reviewed ("Candidate Pool")

The architecture of a digital library adds complexity to the concept of a "book," so many of the terms used to describe objects being reviewed do not in fact make it easy to talk about "how many books were reviewed." In order to accurately associate rights codes with a specific physical object and to reduce duplicate reviewing of different copies of the same item, CRMS makes use of metadata to distinguish relationships. The nature of these relationships often makes it difficult to accurately count "books" as a statistic. Instead we deal with unique scanned objects that become eligible or ineligible for system consideration based on their accompanying metadata. (The following definitions build on each other and thus are presented in conceptual order rather than alphabetically.)

Volume: A volume in HathiTrust is not a "book" in the normal sense of that word but a unit of measurement indicating the unique scan representing one physical item. In line with common library binding practice, it may represent a discrete monograph, a single volume from a monographic series, or several items bound together. Scans of the same work but from different physical copies are treated as unique volumes, and each one receives its own volume ID. Copyright determinations are made at the volume level.

Volume ID: The volume ID is an alphanumeric identifier assigned by HathiTrust and Zephir to a volume (e.g., mdp.39015005731453). Each scan representing a different physical copy of a work is assigned a unique volume ID.

Figure 4 A breakdown of the component parts of a Volume ID

TECHNICAL

 Zephir is a bibliographic metadata management system the California Digital Library developed specifically for HathiTrust. Prior to Zephir's launch in fall 2013, HathiTrust had relied on Mirlyn, the University of Michigan's online catalog.

Catalog ID: The catalog ID is a unique identifier assigned by HathiTrust and Zephir that joins together related volume IDs of a particular work in the same edition. Each catalog ID in Zephir may have one or more than one volume ID associated with it, depending on how many copies of that work in that same edition are in HathiTrust. This relationship can be used to assign rights codes to duplicate volumes; however, a catalog ID may also represent volumes in a multipart monograph. In this case, the catalog ID does not indicate volumes that are exactly the same and should not be used for rights code inheritance without determination of individual parts.

Catalog ID #006155345
- njp.32101066478221
- uc1.b4103074
- uc2.ark:/13960/t7xk8gq25

Catalog ID represents volumes that are the same book, same edition but contributed by different libraries.

Figure 5 Relationship between a Catalog ID and Volume IDs

TECHNICAL

 A common question that arises with a copyright determination project is "How many specific titles or books have been opened by the project?" Providing an answer to this question is complicated due to the one-to-many relationship between catalog IDs and volume IDs in Zephir. This relationship makes it difficult to Identify the specific number of titles opened, because the number of volumes associated with a given catalog record can vary widely. For a given catalog ID, the developer may need to identify which of its associated volume IDs are the same work and which volume IDs are not. Enum/chron metadata will provide important clues to help in making these identifications.

Candidates (pool): The candidates pool is a subset of volumes within HathiTrust whose metadata (date and place of publication, country of origin, current rights, etc.) indicate they are within scope for a defined CRMS copyright review project. The candidates pool will trend toward zero as work progresses; however, it may remain level or even increase as HathiTrust ingests new volumes that match the scope. Candidates are updated each night by a query run against the HathiTrust Rights Database. In some cases, volumes are dropped from candidates due to a change in eligibility often stemming from a correction to their bibliographic metadata.

Active volume: A volume in the candidates queue becomes active whenever someone reviews it. Active volumes are given precedence by the queuing algorithm because work has already been done on them. A volume ceases to be active when all parts of the review process are complete.

Source volume: A source volume is the specific scan that has undergone manual review. A volume ID represents the source volume. Once one copy is reviewed in CRMS and becomes a source volume, then all the other copies associated with that particular catalog ID in

TECHNICAL

Zephir may become "inheriting volumes," provided there is no indication of enum/chron (enumeration and chronology) in the catalog ID.

Inheriting volume(s): Inheriting volumes are all duplicate copies of a work (in that particular edition) in HathiTrust. After a source volume's rights code is exported to the HathiTrust Rights Database, volumes eligible for inheritance are automatically given the same rights code. Inheritance takes place when a CRMS determination is exported to the Rights Database.

The source volume uc2.ark:/13960/t7xk8gq25 (*A Book of Ghosts,* by Sabine Baring-Gould, 1904) underwent manual review by CRMS on October 17, 2012. After a determination was made on the source volume, other volumes associated with the same catalog ID were eligible for inheriting the same rights code.

Two volumes were eligible for inheritance from this source volume: uc1.b4103074 and njp.32101066478221. Inheritance occurred because they were associated with the same catalog ID: Catalog ID #006155345.

One volume was not eligible for inheritance from the source volume because it was a different edition of that work and associated with Catalog ID #006810633 instead. This different edition must be reviewed separately to be given a rights code.

If an institution later joins HathiTrust and if its collection includes a copy of this work in this same edition, then that work will also inherit this rights determination and add to the number of "inheriting volumes" of that work in the digital library.

```
{
    records: {
        "006155345": {
            recordURL: http://catalog.hathitrust.org/Record/006155345,
            titles: [
                "A book of ghosts /",
                "book of ghosts /"
            ],
            isbns: [ ],
            issns: [ ],
            oclcs: [
                "20916821"
            ],
            lccns: [ ],
            publishDates: [
                "1904"
            ]
        }
    },
    items: [
        {
            orig: "Princeton University",
            fromRecord: "006155345",
            htid: "njp.32101066478221",
            itemURL: http://hdl.handle.net/2027/njp.32101066478221,
            rightsCode: "pdus",
            lastUpdate: "20130804",
            enumcron: false,
            usRightsString: "Full view"
        },
        {
            orig: "University of California",
            fromRecord: "006155345",
            htid: "uc1.b4103074",
            itemURL: http://hdl.handle.net/2027/uc1.b4103074,
            rightsCode: "pdus",
            lastUpdate: "20130804",
            enumcron: false,
            usRightsString: "Full view"
        },
        {
            orig: "University of California",
            fromRecord: "006155345",
            htid: "uc2.ark:/13960/t7xk8gq25",
            itemURL: http://hdl.handle.net/2027/uc2.ark:/13960/t7xk8gq25,
            rightsCode: "pdus",
            lastUpdate: "20130811",
            enumcron: false,
            usRightsString: "Full view"
        }
    ]
}
```

Figure 6 Inheritance IDs

Inserts: Component parts in a larger work that were written or created by other authors and may be subject to different copyright terms. Illustrations, articles, quotations, lyrics, and diagrams are examples of "component parts" that could turn out to be inserts. An insert could be an extensive part of a larger work, but even a brief insert can be significant. The presence of an insert is one of the more common reasons why a CRMS reviewer may decide a volume should be set aside as "undetermined."

Multipart monograph: A work composed of more than one part in which the parts have been published over a span of time (usually several years). A multipart monograph can be a special problem in copyright determination because the parts of the work may be subject to different copyright laws—for example, a US work in which the first part was published in 1920, the second part in 1925, and the third in 1930. As a result, the individual parts have to be reviewed independently, even though technically they belong to the same work.

Enum/chron (enumeration and chronology): These are standard metadata used in library catalogs for serial publications and multipart monographs. The presence of enum/chron metadata in a record prevents inheritance of rights codes in CRMS because volumes that are part of a multipart monograph may be subject to different rights.

2. User Roles

Roles are the basis for determining the kinds of privileges people have within CRMS, the interface features available to them, and the levels of access they have to works in the system. In some cases a person may have more than one role.

Reviewer/advanced reviewer: A reviewer is a person authorized to perform copyright determinations. A reviewer is moved up to the status of an advanced reviewer after demonstrating consistent and reliable understanding of the process. Advanced status requires less oversight of a reviewer's work.

TECHNICAL

Expert reviewer: An expert reviewer is a reviewer who is specially trained to adjudicate conflicting reviews. Experts are selected from top-performing reviewers to address conflicts generated by reviewers.

External admin: An external admin is a liaison from a partner institution that may not have authorization to perform copyright determinations but requires access to performance statistics of reviewers from their institution in order to make supervisory decisions.

Admin: An admin is someone entitled to see all project dashboards, statistics, and user information in order to run the project, assess performance, and track activity. An admin cannot override the constraints of the system to change the rights status of a volume.

Super admin: A super admin has the highest level of permissions and may override system logic in order to review any volume, not constrained by the scope of any given candidate pool. Formal legal training is a consideration in granting this role. The system developer also has this role.

3. Interface and System

PageTurner: A HathiTrust application that enables authorized reviewers to view scanned page images. CRMS embeds a version of PageTurner in its interface, but it is a separate application owned and maintained by HathiTrust. HathiTrust access and authentication modules confirm when a user should have authorization to have access to it. If a request for access does not come from an approved IP address, PageTurner will restrict access to works in the public domain. For more details about the application, see http://www.hathitrust.org/access_determination.

Priority: Priority codes route a volume through the CRMS system so it will be displayed to the appropriate user and in some cases restricted from view to other users. The majority of volumes are given Priority 0, which enables any reviewer to see them. Some volumes receive higher priority to ensure they will be reviewed more quickly and/or by a more experienced reviewer.

Status: Status codes indicate how far a volume has progressed through the review process and, to some degree, which path that volume is taking through the system (e.g., Did both reviewers agree or disagree?). Each volume in the queue has a status code, with 0 being the default. The following are the status codes used currently in CRMS-World. Note that Status 1 was not used during the early development of CRMS, and this practice persisted. Volumes progress from Status 0 to another category depending on the result of the review process.

Status	Short explanation
0	Awaiting review or not yet processed
2	Conflict
3	Match pending expert review
4	Match
5	Reviewed by expert
6	HathiTrust issue reported
7	Status 3 expert review completed
8	Partial match resolved by system
9	System-generated review for rights inheritance

Validation/invalidation rate: A validation rate is the percentage of an individual's reviews that either matched other reviewers' judgments or are deemed correct by experts. The statistic is represented as validation in the personal display. For the management team, it displays in the converse as invalidation. The validation rate is a broad measurement to test how closely a reviewer is aligned with the CRMS review process. Adjudications where an expert elects to apply the Swiss option do not count against a reviewer's validation rate.

Instead, they are counted separately, influencing neither validation nor invalidation.

Swiss option: The Swiss option is an alternative to invalidation, which an expert reviewer may employ during adjudication to grant a neutral mark to a nonconforming review. Without this option, any reviews that do not match the expert's would count as errors in the reviewer's personal statistics. A Swiss option neutralizes the issue and avoids invalidating either reviewer. It is primarily useful in situations where there is complexity or a judgment call beyond the bounds of routine work.

4. Rights Determination

Review: A review is an individual reviewer's judgment about the copyright status of a work. The reason for that judgment is stored in the system with a corresponding rights code. Depending on how a volume moves through the CRMS process, two or three reviews may accrue before a final determination is reached.

Conflict: A conflict occurs when two reviews for a volume disagree on one or more critical pieces of information that would affect access to the work. For example, two independent reviews of the same work are in conflict where one reviewer selects "public domain" and the other selects "in copyright."

Final determination: A final determination is the collective result of all reviews done on a volume (including, if necessary, an expert's adjudication). It is the result when that process is complete.

Exported determinations: Not all final determinations are sent to the HathiTrust Rights Database. Exported determinations are a subset of final determinations that meet criteria for export.

Be wary of export determinations that might close works that should be open. The distinction between "final" and "exported" determinations became necessary in CRMS-World because certain und/nfi determinations would override a preexisting pdus determination in HathiTrust.

As an example of how this could happen, consider that the scope of the CRMS-World project includes some Australian, Canadian, and British works that were published before 1923. Some percentages of these were found to be und/nfi by CRMS reviewers. However, under US copyright law, works published prior to 1923 are pd or (at the very least) pdus. If CRMS-World were to export a und/nfi determination for a pre-1923 work to the Rights Database, that would close the work in the United States as well as in its country of origin. To ensure this does not happen, CRMS does not export such determinations to the Rights Database (though a record of the und/nfi judgment will be kept in the CRMS database).

TECHNICAL

Attribute: A rights code is composed of two parts. The first half is called the attribute, and it represents the copyright status of the work and facilitates access control. Examples of attributes used by CRMS are "ic," "icus," "pd," "pdus," and "und." There are twenty-six attributes (as of this writing), though most are not used in copyright determination. A list of attributes can be found at http://www.hathitrust.org/rights_database.

Reason: A rights code is composed of two parts. The second half is called the "reason," and it accounts for why the volume was given that copyright status. There are eighteen "reasons" (as of this writing) accounting for a number of different situations. A list of reasons can be found at http://www.hathitrust.org/rights_database.

Rights code: A shorthand term representing both the attribute and reason code of a determination.

Rights database: The repository of rights information for each digitized volume in HathiTrust. The Rights Database should not be confused with the CRMS database, which is a separate repository that includes more detailed metadata necessary for rights research. For further details, see https://www.hathitrust.org/rights_database.

TECHNICAL

TECHNICAL COMPONENTS

A rights determination system is complex because it must meet stringent requirements pertaining to copyright law, security best practices, reliable data management, and flexible user management and access. This section will provide a detailed discussion of the system components we have implemented to address these concerns.

At its core, CRMS is a web-hosted application using MySQL as a data store. Two database tables are especially important: the queue and the review table. The queue is the set of volumes waiting for or in the process of review, and the review table stores the data entered by users submitting reviews. Data in both tables are moved to other database tables when the review process is completed, so these tables are constantly in flux.

The review interface embeds many research resources within its limited screen real estate. When a reviewer visits the interface, the queuing algorithm automatically assigns volumes for review and ensures that two different users review each volume. If there is a disagreement, then an expert resolves the conflict with a third review. Finally, the resulting copyright determinations are exported to the HathiTrust Rights Database daily.

This section has been divided into three parts: "Core Elements," "Critical Advanced Elements," and "Recommended Elements." Core elements are essential to the rights determination process and must be included in any copyright review project. Critical advanced elements, while not essential to the rights determination process as such, are necessary to maintain the security and efficiency of a rights determination system at scale. Recommended elements are valuable features that further improve the system's flexibility, efficiency, and usability.

CORE ELEMENTS

Web-Based Application Infrastructure

CRMS was designed as a web-based application so that trained librarians and staff at partner institutions could access a secure, hosted space on the University of Michigan infrastructure and participate in copyright determination. Users can access the CRMS interface via commonly used browsers, including Firefox, Chrome, or Opera. This approach allows us to be platform agnostic.

> The alternative to a web-based application would have been a downloadable native application. However, this would have forced us to either (1) require a specific operating system or (2) attempt cross platform development, a daunting prospect when development resources are limited. Such a decentralized approach would also have made keeping users' software up to date very challenging.

The underlying code of CRMS is composed of Perl CGI scripts and JavaScript. The various displayed pages of the interface are created using Template Toolkit (http://www.template-toolkit.org) because it integrates seamlessly with Perl.

> The CRMS code is reliable thanks to over six years of modification and debugging, but the choice to use Perl was decided largely due to its common use in development projects at the time. If we were building CRMS today, Rails would be a likely alternative because the University of Michigan Library considers it a "best practices" platform for new development. The CRMS pages are relatively static, requiring only an occasional AJAX-style callback to a server for additional computation (e.g., when calculating a rights prediction based on an author's death date in CRMS-World). Most "web languages," such as Python or Ruby, would be appropriate for building a CRMS-style system.

CRMS Database

The CRMS database stores and provides access to review and determination results within the system. In addition to the queue and review table, CRMS also stores a candidate pool (volumes that will eventually be in the queue), historical reviews that have already been used to make copyright determinations, and data on those determinations. There are various secondary tables that also store precalculated (to reduce page load times) statistics on system and user activity.

The database also stores selected bibliographic metadata—including title, author, publication date, country of publication, and a catalog ID—without a significant increase to the database's storage footprint. While this information is available outside CRMS, there are two reasons we keep some metadata locally. The first is data locality: it is an order of magnitude slower to retrieve metadata via the HathiTrust Bibliographic API. The second is that the information is often used in SQL queries, where the metadata is searched via a JOIN. These selected metadata are sufficient for daily use by reviewers; higher-latency calls to the Bibliographic API are made from overnight processes that are not performance-critical.

MySQL has been a reliable database management system for a user base of over fifty reviewers contributing hundreds of reviews each day; it has also been seamless in handling complex queries across large tables. MySQL has full support in the University of Michigan Library infrastructure, where it is considered significantly easier to maintain than Oracle.

The most important thing for the developer to keep in mind when working on database communication is to follow—to the greatest extent possible—best security practices in sanitizing all external inputs. CRMS follows the practice of using "bind parameters" with Perl's DBI drivers.

TECHNICAL

An obvious question during the design of CRMS-World was whether it should have a completely separate codebase or whether the architecture of CRMS-US could be extended to handle CRMS-World workflow. The design team decided the latter approach would be more expedient, though it did impose a limit on metadata collection. CRMS-US had two database fields for Stanford copyright renewal data. CRMS-World repurposed these two fields to store author death dates and publication information. This compromise had the unfortunate side effect of directly supporting only one machine-readable author death date per volume. An alternate option would have been to design a mechanism that allowed the input of more than one contributor (including authors, editors, illustrators, etc.). An additional database table can hold this information, but providing multiple data entry fields to support it can be a challenge if screen real estate is limited.

Algorithms/Heuristics for Identifying Which Works Are In-Scope

Large digital libraries such as HathiTrust include works that are subject to different copyright regimes depending on their country of origin and other factors. The project will need heuristics and algorithms to translate the goals of the rights determination project into a reasonably sized "pool of candidates" for copyright review. If the project is ongoing and the candidate pool is open-ended, the algorithms must also identify works that have recently become candidates as a result of new library accessions. CRMS relies on time stamps from the HathiTrust Rights Database to identify volumes added or modified since the previous check.

The bibliographic metadata of volumes in the digital library is used to determine which of them will be in scope for the project. The review system requires access to that metadata, including publication date, country of origin, and/or others as appropriate for the copyright regime in question. The developer may find it helpful to have access to someone with cataloging expertise to aid in parsing record formats like MARC.

> Using the MARC record to identify the publication date for a volume can present particularly difficult challenges. For example, the MARC 008 fixed field contains subfields, including DateType, Date1, and Date2. The DateType byte contains one of fifteen possible codes to indicate how the other fields are to be interpreted. This required considerable attention to detail in early CRMS versions. Ultimately, CRMS adopted HathiTrust's copyright date algorithm, which makes correct use of all three fields. For more information, see http://www.hathitrust.org/bib_rights_determination.

Another issue for CRMS-World concerned date ranges in the MARC 008 fixed field. Each volume of a multivolume or multiyear work potentially has its own date among the enum/chron metadata, and together these dates might be represented on the catalog record in the form of a range. The project team discussed the possibility of trying to parse a single publication date from the enum/chron metadata, but we were not able to find a reliable method for translating human-readable enum/chron metadata into a machine-readable form. We decided instead to exclude volumes with ranges for publication dates from our candidate pool.

A Queuing Algorithm That Presents the Right Volumes to the Right People

CRMS was designed with a separate queue and candidate pool—the former being much smaller than the latter—for the sake of having greater flexibility to customize the presentation of volumes to reviewers without the potential inefficiency of manipulating a large database table. So long as the queue is set at a size beyond what reviewers can reasonably accomplish in a single day, it can be repopulated from the pool each night with no negative impact on productivity.

The most important tasks for the CRMS queuing algorithm are to (1) make sure the same user does not review the same volume twice, (2) prioritize volumes that already have one review, and (3) prevent volumes from receiving more than the required two reviews.[67]

The algorithm uses a locking mechanism to prevent simultaneous review. It "locks" a volume (setting a flag in the queue entry for the volume) whenever a reviewer is working on it and unlocks it when the review is submitted. This prevents a third reviewer from seeing the volume during its second review. And because the algorithm always checks review counts, a volume cannot be presented again after its second review.

---

[67] We specify two rather than three because the queuing algorithm does not control an expert's adjudication.

The queuing algorithm also controls other noncore functions, including priority and projects (both discussed below).

Review Interface with Information Resources Appropriate to the Research

The review interface provides a scanned view of the work and allows the reviewer to enter information relevant to that work's copyright status. It also allows the reviewer either to confirm the system's recommended rights determination or to select a different determination based on additional information discovered during the review.

TECHNICAL

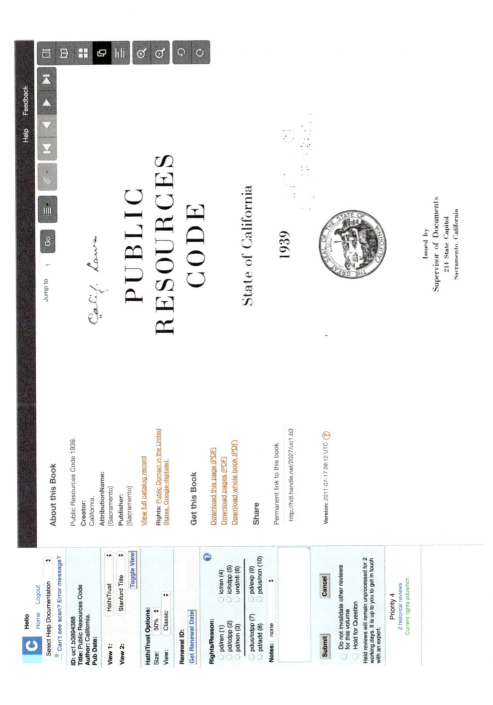

Figure 7 CRMS-US interface

Figure 8 CRMS-World interface

The left side of the interface (the "operational pane") displays a summary of the volume's bibliographic metadata, options for adjusting the display of the scan and for setting display defaults, and radio buttons for selecting a rights determination. A text box and a drop-down menu with note categories allow the reviewer to add notes about the volume, including additional author death dates or possible inserts.

The interface streamlines the review process by providing single-click access to online resources such as the Virtual International Authority File (VIAF), the Library of Congress Authorities, and Wikipedia. In CRMS, the reviewer can toggle between a view of the scanned volume and a view of a selected resource with a single click. If an embedded resource has a discoverable URL scheme, it can be "presearched" for the user by crafting a URL based on bibliographic information. This means that search results of system-generated keywords are already displayed by the time the interface is toggled to the resource. Almost all the resources available in CRMS support this feature.

CRMS stores the URLs of these information sources as templates in a database table. Embedded placeholders like __AUTHOR__ are replaced with actual bibliographic data as the review interface is being constructed. This approach—storing resources in a database table or config file—has the additional benefit of making possible on-the-fly adjustments because third-party websites occasionally drift over time.

A Way to Export Determinations

A mechanism is needed in order to make determinations available for use. What form that mechanism takes depends on the way your institution implements rights determinations.

In the case of CRMS, there was already a HathiTrust protocol for submitting text files with rights determinations for automatic processing. The submission format is a simple tab-delimited file that contains the rights attribute, reason, and originating system (CRMS-US or CRMS-World). This provided a convenient way for CRMS to share determinations with the HathiTrust Rights Database.

A consequence of this approach (as opposed to having the HathiTrust database request determinations via an API) is that the CRMS database is a "black box" to the outside world. The HathiTrust database receives rights determinations, but it cannot access other metadata (such as author death dates) that would explain or justify those determinations.

If the decision is made to implement an API, developers will need to consider carefully which data can be queried. Sensitive data, such as personally identifying information, must be protected. Access controls around the API must conform to institutional policy.

CRITICAL ADVANCED ELEMENTS

While not core to the rights determination process, the following elements are extremely important for any copyright determination project and should be included in the system's design.

Appropriate Access Controls

Rights determination projects by definition require access to potentially copyrighted works, so their design must give the highest priority to restricting access to that material only to authorized reviewers.

This may not be a simple task. Access control in copyright determination systems will need to achieve three major goals:

1. Seamless integration of the review system and the digital library, both of which may have their own authentication systems with different levels of authorization
2. Management of users having a variety of privileges
3. Reliable and secure export of rights determination data from the review system to the digital library

Developers are accustomed to dealing with security concerns, but copyright determination will be subject to particularly intense scrutiny from rights holders concerned about the protection of copyrighted material. Even experienced users find navigating through multiple layers of access challenging, but the design team may only be able to streamline that experience to a limited degree. Reviewers will need carefully worded, step-by-step instructions—and possibly online user support—to guide them through the authorization process.

In the case of CRMS, there are five broad levels of access:

1. The library system (U-M Library, the host infrastructure for the other layers)
2. The review system (CRMS)
3. Content subject to copyright (hosted in HathiTrust)
4. Administrative functions (in CRMS, accessible only to developers and administrators)
5. Development system (in CRMS, accessible only to developers and testers)

A user's access depends on the user's status among the CRMS user types. The list below details the set of user privileges within CRMS; it is not strictly a hierarchy. Significant privileges (especially access to copyrighted material) are extended only to users who require them. Access to in-copyright works and the ability to submit reviews are the most tightly controlled privileges and extended only when necessary.

- *Reviewer.* A new user who has recently completed training and is in a probationary period. If the two reviews for a volume are both provided by new reviewers, their work is double-checked by an expert even if their judgments match. This provides an

additional degree of oversight for users who are still in the learning process.
- *Advanced reviewer.* This designation is for reviewers who have fully completed their training process. Experts do not adjudicate advanced reviewer judgments unless they conflict.
- *Expert (or "expert reviewer").* Experts are chosen when they exhibit sufficient experience and mastery of process to adjudicate conflicts between reviewers and advanced reviewers. Experts receive additional training before being assigned this privilege.
- *External admin.* Reserved for supervisors at partner institutions who wish to monitor the progress of their own reviewers. An external admin can view statistics of all reviewers at their institution but cannot view information about any other reviewers and cannot submit reviews.
- *Admin.* The access level extended to members of the project team. This privilege includes access to statistics for all reviewers and the ability to add volumes to the queue.
- *Super admin.* The highest level of access that may be necessary for the primary developer and the project's principal investigator. Functionality exposed by this privilege is primarily used for debugging and is only rarely used.

Each page in the CRMS system has a database entry that indicates the privilege level required to access it. The links displayed on the CRMS main page and in the navigation menus are tailored for each user, displaying only those pages they are authorized to visit. To prevent a technically adept user from manually crafting a URL they are not authorized to visit, the main CGI script performs an additional privilege check before serving the requested page.

Some pages are sensitive to user privilege in terms of the actions they are allowed to carry out there. For example, some pages allow viewing but not editing of information unless the user has additional privileges.

An Algorithm to Provide Recommended Judgments

The workflow of a rights determination project is based on the copyright laws applicable to the works under review. In most cases, copyright duration is based on the life of the author plus a specific number of years. When assessing whether a particular volume has entered the public domain, a limited number of mathematical calculations are necessary. Individual reviewers can perform these, but a better option is to translate the law into algorithms when possible.

For CRMS-World, we introduced an algorithm that selects the appropriate rights code for reviewers after they have entered sufficient information to make the prediction. This has the advantage of freeing reviewers from doing date arithmetic and encapsulating the logic in a program that can be carefully inspected to ensure correctness. For example, when determining the public domain status for a single-author work published in the UK, our system can take the death date of the author of the volume and apply the UK's "life of the author + 70 years" copyright duration to the work.

Since a copyright in a single-author work continues until the last day of the "life + 70" term, the first year a work enters the public domain is actually the "year of the author's death + 71." This is a textbook example of something that should be done algorithmically to avoid inevitable "off by one" errors by reviewers.

When a work passes through CRMS-World, the system's recommended judgment is visible to the reviewer in the interface. The reviewer can either confirm that recommendation or decide to change it based on additional information discovered during the review. The presence of third-party authored material (i.e., inserts) within the work is the most common situation that prompts the reviewer to override the system recommendation.

A Mechanism for Resolving Conflicting Reviews

Any system that employs a two-review process will generate conflicting reviews and should have a mechanism for addressing them. Resolving conflicts helps maintain the integrity of the copyright review process and provides an opportunity to educate reviewers when their reviews fall outside of accepted practice. Conflict resolution can be accomplished through the oversight of an expert reviewer.

Copyright review at a large scale results in hundreds of daily determinations. Managing conflicts can quickly become a grueling process unless experts have a mechanism for organizing and working with relevant conflicting reviews. In the case of CRMS, we provided a "conflicts page"

TECHNICAL

for aggregating reviews in conflict so the experts can easily adjudicate them and give them final determinations.

The CRMS approach to conflicts has evolved over time; reviews of a work must agree on the rights attribute ("public domain" or "in copyright"), but our systems do not require them to match in every detail (e.g., author death dates, copyright renewal numbers, and dates). Expert reviewers are only required to address conflicts when their resolution will determine whether a volume will be opened or remain closed. This has the effect of significantly reducing an expert reviewer's workload without compromising the reliability of the review process.

Conflicts that do not have an impact on access can be left for resolution in the future. For example, if a conflict involves only ic and und attributes, the system automatically gives it a und/crms final determination. This acknowledges the fact that no matter which attribute the expert would have selected (ic or und), exporting the determination to the Rights Database would have the same result: the work remains closed.

RECOMMENDED ELEMENTS

Recommended elements are valuable features that further improve the system's flexibility, efficiency, and usability.

TECHNICAL

A Way to Link a Given Determination with a Set of Reviews

If reviews and their associated determinations are stored in separate tables, it is useful to have an explicit identifier linking them. CRMS uses an auto-incrementing group identifier to associate all the reviews that contributed to a determination. Use of a "foreign key" such as this is common in database programming. Since volumes do occasionally get re-reviewed (case in point, when the copyright term expires), it is necessary to be able to distinguish unambiguously the reviews that contributed to each determination without resorting to fuzzy time stamp logic.

A Means for Reviewers to Put Their Review Temporarily "On Hold"

A hold period allows a reviewer to temporarily set aside a partially completed review in order to submit a question to the project team about a point of copyright law or some other part of the research process. Once the reviewer has an answer, the review is easy to retrieve, edit, and submit. The hold period should allow a reasonable span of time for the project team to respond to the matter in question.

CRMS implements this feature with a "hold" time stamp field in the review database record. To prevent a reviewer from repeatedly holding and unholding the review (which would prevent the volume from being processed and finalized), a second field with a "sticky" value retains the original hold date, and the system applies it if the reviewer later attempts to place a hold on her review. The hold mechanism prevents overnight processing from assigning a status (i.e., match versus conflict) to the queued volume but does not prevent the volume from being presented to a second reviewer.

A related benefit of the system's hold feature is a grace period between the submission of a review and the system processing it that evening. A reviewer may make changes or add information to her reviews at any point prior to overnight processing (when her review will be matched with other reviews for that volume).

Inheriting Rights Determinations on Otherwise Identical Volumes

A mechanism to minimize duplicative review effort is important when working with large-scale collections. CRMS attempts to keep only one representative volume from a catalog record in the candidate pool. Once a determination is made for that volume, other volumes associated with that catalog record are eligible to inherit the same determination.

If new volumes are added to your project, it is important to identify those that have already been reviewed. A second form of inheritance, "candidate inheritance," applies when a volume enters the candidate pool either because it was recently ingested by HathiTrust or due to a bibliographic correction. The system searches for other volumes' completed determinations on the same catalog record, and if it finds that a determination already exists, then the new volume is eligible to inherit that determination. The new candidate can be removed, as there is no need for a review.

> The inheritance process is automatic but subject to constraints. For example, inheritance is disallowed when the catalog record indicates that the volume is likely to be part of a multipart monograph or similar series. Experts are required to approve inheritances in some cases.

A "Subproject" Mechanism That Allows Assignment of Volumes and Reviewers to Specific Sets of Works for Review

At the beginning of a copyright review project, reviewers are frequently tasked with performing one type of review on a single pool of candidates. Our experience has been that librarians, users, and administrators may identify specific populations of works for review, which must be prioritized and reviewed separately from the main candidate pool. Consequently, your project team may be asked to take on special subprojects featuring their own candidate pools.

The "subproject" mechanism allows us to select specific volumes for separate review only by a designated subset of reviewers. Once defined, administrators should be able to assign reviewers to a given subproject based on criteria appropriate for that project. This may in some cases mean a reviewer could be assigned to more than one subproject. Some projects may require a narrower, more specialized group of reviewers. For example, a subproject composed of Spanish works may be best suited for reviewers with fluency in Spanish.

When implementing a "subproject" mechanism, there are other considerations to keep in mind. These will have implications for both the queue and the candidate pool of each project:

1. If candidacy requirements can be distilled into an algorithm based on bibliographic metadata, then volumes can be added to a subproject's candidate pool automatically.
2. Alternatively, a subproject may be populated from some other source, such as a patron-provided spreadsheet explicitly listing volume identifiers that are in scope for that subproject.
3. It is necessary to have a well-articulated policy for dealing with exhaustion of a subproject reviewer's pool. The reviewer should be alerted when moving from one subproject to another, so that they do not misapply one subproject's process to a different candidate pool. While it is possible to create a fallback mechanism that queues nonsubproject candidates once a given subproject pool is exhausted, it would be preferable to require the reviewer to take a specific action to move from one queue to another.

TECHNICAL

A Mechanism to Detect When Re-review Is Likely to Be Profitable

A work identified as in copyright by a rights determination project can be scheduled for re-review when its metadata indicate it has crossed a date boundary that may put it in the public domain. If your project collects author death dates and/or publication dates, it will be possible to conduct an annual search of previously determined volumes and identify those that have likely entered the public domain. Those eligible can then be queued for re-review.

Tools for Searching Various Categories of Reviews

Search features in a copyright review system must allow reviewers and administrators to find volumes and reviews using selected criteria. These search features should include historical reviews (i.e., finished and exported) and unprocessed reviews (i.e., still editable). Users rely on these tools to refresh their memories when reviewing a volume with an issue similar to one they encountered before. These tools can also aid self-training by allowing reviewers to consult expert adjudication notes. Finally, access to unprocessed reviews allows reviewers to find and edit their reviews from earlier in the day.

TECHNICAL

copyright review management system

| Home | Review | Search/Browse | Documentation | Stats/Reports | Administrative |

logout
Click here to report errors
CRMS version 5.2.3

Historical Reviews:

Search for: Reviews ▾ where
Attribute ▾ und AND ▾
Identifier ▾ AND ▾
Identifier ▾
Start Date: (YYYY-MM-DD)
End Date: (YYYY-MM-DD)
Order by: Identifier ▾
Direction: Ascending ▾
Display: 20 records per page.
Submit Clear

Search Help / Search Terms

Found 194472 reviews for 107777 volumes, page 1 of 9724
previous 20 || next 20 || first page || last page   download ☐ Show Additional Fields

ID	Title	Author	Pub Date	Review Date	Status	Legacy	Reviewer	Attr	Reason	Note Category	Note	Priority	Verdict	Swiss
bc.ark:/13960/t0cv6qg3n	Woman's duties in social and political life.	Pius XII, Pope	1945	2014-03-21	4	0		und	nfi	Foreign Author	Pius XII, Pope, 1876-1958 IT - Italy	0	✓	0
bc.ark:/13960/t0cv6qg3n	Woman's duties in social and political life.	Pius XII, Pope	1945	2014-03-21	4	0		und	nfi	Foreign Author	Pius Xii, Pope, 1876-1958 ; IT - Italy	0	✓	0
bc.ark:/13960/t1bk3mc4g	On Mother's Day.		1952	2014-03-21	5	0	[Reviewer names redacted.]	und	nfi	Insert(s)	multiple authors, material within is attributed	0	✓	0
bc.ark:/13960/t1bk3mc4g	On Mother's Day.		1952	2014-03-24	5	0		und	nfi	Insert(s)	most pieces included attributed to individual authors	0	✓	1
bc.ark:/13960/t1mg9xg3s	The Rosary Crusade		1943	2014-03-21	5	0		und	nfi	Insert(s)	permission note (verso)	0	✓	0
bc.ark:/13960/t1mg9xg3s	The Rosary Crusade		1943	2014-03-24	5	0		und	nfi	Insert(s)	permission including on verso	0	✓	1
bc.ark:/13960/t1wd4vm14	Oration	Lyons, Charles W.	1923	2012-08-30	4	0		und	nfi	Not Class A	"oration" : speech : "Delivered before the ...."--T.p.	0	✓	0
bc.ark:/13960/t1wd4vm14	Oration	Lyons, Charles W.	1923	2012-08-30	4	0		und	nfi	Not Class A	t.p. says this was delivered before the City Government ...	0	✓	0
bc.ark:/13960/t2990nm81	Madonna of the Americas	Garza, Hildebrando.	1954	2014-03-21	5	0		und	nfi	Insert(s)	Madonna of the Americas by Don Hildebrando Garza, O.S.B. Mexico City, is a reprint from Sponsa Regis, May, 1954.	0	✓	0
bc.ark:/13960/t2990nm81	Madonna of the Americas	Garza, Hildebrando.	1954	2014-03-24	5	0		und	nfi	Insert(s)	reprint of a periodical (likely)	0	✓	1

Figure 9 CRMS-US historical reviews table

Reviewer Performance Statistics Pages

Statistics reports to track reviewers' performance (i.e., validation rates) should be accessible to the reviewers and to their supervisors (i.e., external administrators) at their respective institutions. We found this access helped communicate the importance of CRMS to the supervisors and give them a concrete set of metrics by which to evaluate the work.

	Project Total	Total 2015	Jan 2015	Feb 2015	Mar 2015	Apr 2015	May 2015	Jun 2015	Jul 2015	Aug 2015	Sep 2015	Oct 2015	Nov 2015	Dec 2015
PD Reviews	305788 (52.9%)	16341 (75.5%)	1159 (71.9%)	2067 (71.2%)	2143 (67.6%)	1423 (68.7%)	749 (88.5%)	2596 (95.3%)	1576 (73.5%)	1348 (75.9%)	1119 (77.2%)	1106 (72.6%)	700 (74.5%)	355 (71.1%)
IC Reviews	101437 (17.5%)	65 (0.3%)	4 (0.2%)	16 (0.6%)	8 (0.3%)	4 (0.2%)	0 (0.0%)	0 (0.0%)	11 (0.5%)	1 (0.1%)	6 (0.4%)	3 (0.2%)	8 (0.9%)	4 (0.8%)
UND/NFI Reviews	171063 (29.6%)	5252 (24.2%)	449 (27.9%)	820 (28.2%)	1017 (32.1%)	645 (31.1%)	97 (11.5%)	129 (4.7%)	557 (26.0%)	427 (24.0%)	325 (22.4%)	414 (27.2%)	232 (24.7%)	140 (28.1%)
Total Reviews*	578288	21658	1612	2903	3168	2072	846	2725	2144	1776	1450	1523	940	499
Non-Expert Reviews	534804 (92.5%)	15280 (70.6%)	1229 (76.2%)	2212 (76.2%)	2360 (74.5%)	1637 (79.0%)	518 (61.2%)	1954 (68.4%)	1361 (63.5%)	1255 (70.7%)	1051 (72.5%)	1063 (69.8%)	446 (47.4%)	284 (56.9%)
Neutral Reviews & Rate	17583 (3.3%)	745 (4.9%)	65 (5.3%)	113 (5.1%)	85 (3.6%)	57 (3.5%)	10 (1.9%)	17 (0.9%)	53 (3.9%)	107 (8.5%)	106 (10.1%)	85 (8.0%)	33 (7.4%)	14 (4.9%)
Invalidated Reviews & Rate	13951 (2.6%)	463 (3.0%)	43 (3.5%)	54 (2.4%)	52 (2.2%)	46 (2.8%)	5 (1.0%)	3 (0.2%)	44 (3.2%)	57 (4.5%)	57 (5.4%)	48 (4.5%)	42 (9.4%)	12 (4.2%)
Time Reviewing (mins)	729174	22531	1886	2623	2653	2074	751	2747	2161	2017	1796	1801	1264	758
Time per Review (mins)	1.3	1.1	1.3	1.0	0.9	1.1	1.0	1.1	1.1	1.2	1.4	1.3	1.4	1.7
Reviews per Hour	45.6	53.5	46.8	62.7	69.3	56.9	62.2	55.5	53.4	48.7	43.5	45.3	41.6	34.7
Outlier Reviews	24449	1561	140	164	102	105	67	185	222	140	149	184	63	60

Figure 10 Reviews statistics table

Business intelligence–style dashboards can provide useful statistics for tracking the project. Dashboards can also be a form of advertising, giving potential new participants an opportunity to see what the project has accomplished in a form that is appealing and easy to understand.

TECHNICAL

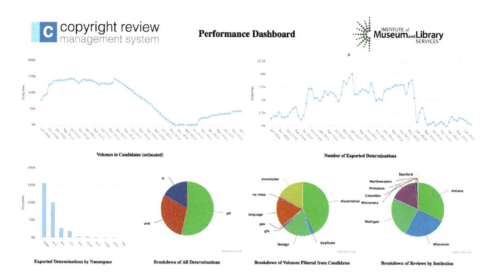

Figure 11 CRMS-US dashboard

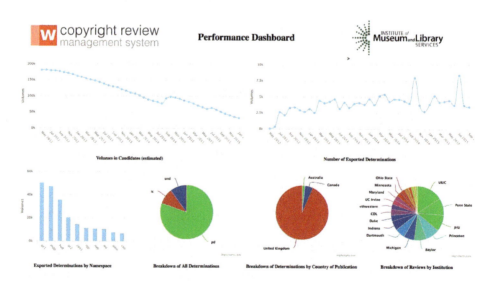

Figure 12 CRMS-World dashboard

Priority

It is occasionally useful to bypass the normal function of the algorithm by prioritizing a volume for review. A priority system in the queue allows administrators to accelerate review of one or more volumes to respond to time-sensitive requests. In general, having fine-grained priority levels grants nuanced control over volumes as they move through the review process. As part of this, it is likely that an interface for administrators to manually add volumes to the queue will be useful.

A Mechanism for Overseeing New Reviewer Performance

It may be useful to oversee reviewers who have recently completed training to ensure their early reviews consistently reflect the project's established standards. Newly trained reviewers can use a "Provisional Match" page so experts can evaluate their work.

TRAINING SANDBOX

The sandbox is an additional tool used to bring new reviewers into the CRMS system. It allows new reviewers to practice performing reviews without affecting the CRMS live production space.

These are criteria for selecting single, complete, correct reviews from the production site to be imported into the training site. Generally the degree to which a trainee disagrees with the existing review is a progress indicator. This is particularly true for those production reviews that an expert reviewer has vetted. However, both Status 4 and 5 reviews are eligible for import.

The program that imports reviews takes a parameter indicating how many reviews to import. Historically we have imported on the order of one thousand to two thousand at a time. This appears to have been sufficient, given the trainee cadre sizes we have seen in several rounds of training.

The most recent reviews in production are considered first. A review qualifies for sandbox import if it satisfies all the following requirements:

- It has a final determination (i.e., is in historical reviews).
- It is Status 4 or 5.
- It is marked as correct.
- It is by a user with subexpert privileges (i.e., a peer).
- The volume has no Swiss reviews.
- The determination was not */crms (i.e., a und/ic hybrid).
- Neither the volume's author nor title have been encountered on any other volume imported in this round.

THE CRMS REVIEW PROCESSES

This part of the technical section addresses how the technical components described above work together in practice. Here we present the review process in a roughly chronological form, moving from

TECHNICAL

our methods for identifying review candidate volumes through to the export of CRMS determinations. Given its focus on the practical application of CRMS, this part will also identify and describe a few noteworthy differences between the CRMS-US and CRMS-World projects.

Zephir and the HathiTrust Rights Database

For a work to be reviewed by CRMS, it must first be included in HathiTrust and in Zephir (HathiTrust's "bibliographic metadata management system," which can be accessed through the digital library's online catalog). At present, there are over thirteen million volumes in Zephir. Given the size of HathiTrust, the CRMS project had to take precaution when establishing the scope of our inquiry or risk having a pool of candidates beyond the limits of even our well-funded effort.

An equally important resource for CRMS is the HathiTrust Rights Database, which tracks each volume's current rights status as well as any changes to its status. Due to the "one-to-many" relationship between a catalog record and its component volumes (which may have different rights), the decision was made to keep the data stand-alone, outside the catalog.

CRMS has read-only access to the Rights Database, and this allows CRMS to query the Rights Database for newly deposited or newly changed items that are in scope for rights determination. Each rights entry has a time stamp, so CRMS can limit its query to only the volumes modified or added since its previous query.

Criteria for Identifying In-Scope Volumes

For a copyright review project drawing from a digital library on the scale of HathiTrust, it is essential to develop criteria for selecting volumes to be reviewed.

"Country of origin" was a major influence on the scope of each CRMS project. The chosen country determines which copyright laws will apply to the works in scope, and it also determines the potential size of that pool. The decision of the first CRMS project to focus on works published in the United States between 1923 and 1963 meant we would eventually be dealing with a pool of over three hundred thousand works.

The differences between US copyright law and the laws in Australia, Canada, and the UK meant that different criteria would be needed for the research methods in CRMS-US and CRMS-World. These criteria determined the metadata that each version of CRMS used to create its own pool of candidates.

A volume was a candidate for CRMS-US if it matched the following criteria:

- Rights of "ic/bib" ("in copyright/bibliographically derived by automatic processes")

- Bibliographic format of "bk" (book; MARC leader[6] in {a,t} and leader[7] in {a,c,d,m})[68]
- Published 1923–63 inclusive (based on 008 copyright year)
- Published in the United States (i.e., not a foreign work; based on 008[15-17])
- In English (based on 008[35-37])
- Not a government document (based on a number of heuristics; see appendices)
- Not a translation (041:a set to "eng" and 041:h set to a different language code, or "translat{ion,ed}" found in 245:c or 500:a)
- Not a dissertation ("thes{e,i}s" or "diss" found in 500:a or 502:a)

A volume was a candidate for CRMS-World if it matched the following criteria:

- Rights of "ic/bib" or "pdus/bib"[69]
- Published in Australia, Canada, or the UK[70]

---

68 CRMS-US only reviewed "books." See the HathiTrust page on Bibliographic Rights Determination for more about formats: HathiTrust. "Automated Bibliographic Rights Determination," accessed January 20, 2016, http://www.hathitrust.org/bib_rights_determination.

69 Or those with the attribute "op," but these are less common.

70 This criterion is actually similar to the criterion of "no foreign works" in CRMS-US. In CRMS-World, a "foreign" work is one not published in Australia, Canada, or the UK, so for CRMS-World the United States counts as "foreign" and out-of-scope.

- Published between the following spans[71]
  - 1871–1941 (UK)
  - 1891–1961 (Australia or Canada)
- In English (based on 008[35-37])
- Not a translation (041:a set to "eng" and 041:h set to a different language code, or "translat{ion,ed}" found in 245:c or 500:a)
- Single publication/copyright date (for now; based on 008[6], 008[7-10], and 008[11-14])

The Candidates Pool

When a volume has been identified as a candidate for CRMS review, it must be added to the particular pool of candidates matching its bibliographic criteria. ("Pool" is the term CRMS commonly uses, but "stack" would be more apt, technically.) This is one of several tasks "overnight processing" addresses.

Overnight processing is a script that runs each night in several phases and handles tasks that are important to nearly every step in the CRMS review process, from selecting volumes for review to exporting determinations to the HathiTrust Rights Database.

---

71 Note that the dates are those provided in the CRMS-World proposal to IMLS. The dates moved forward by one each year, so by 2015 the spans were 1875–1945 and 1895–1945, respectively.

TECHNICAL

The overnight processing phase called "candidate import" is responsible for adding volumes to the candidate pool. It first compiles a list of all volumes in the HathiTrust Rights Database that have been added or changed in the previous twenty-four hours. Then it examines each volume's current rights and its bibliographic metadata stored in Zephir. With that information, the system is able to tell whether a volume ought to go through CRMS. If it should, then the system adds the volume to the pool as a candidate and copies relevant parts of its metadata into the CRMS database; otherwise, the logic simply moves on to the next volume. It also occasionally detects when a previously added candidate no longer meets the requirements for candidacy (typically due to a bibliographic metadata correction) and quietly removes it from the pool.

A volume is not allowed into the candidate pool if the system discovers it has been through CRMS already. When a volume has been reviewed, the system adds it to the "historical reviews" database table, so the system will ignore any potential candidates that already have a listing there. If the system is running correctly, there is no way for a previously reviewed volume to get back into CRMS without some kind of human intervention.[72]

---

72 An administrator or expert can manually add a volume back into the CRMS queue, but this is usually done only when a specific issue arises with a volume or when the project team is conducting a formal "re-review" to test the reliability and/or the results of the CRMS process.

Before a volume enters the review process, the system will draw it from the pool of candidates into the queue.

The Queue

The queue is a subset of the candidate pool containing volumes that are next in line for the reviewers. While it is not absolutely necessary for the review process, the queue provides a smaller and more predictable set of volumes, and this makes it easier to work with than the candidate pool itself. The queue can be set to a specific number of volumes and provides an easier target for tracking statistics for daily and monthly reports.

The queue is stored in its own table in the CRMS database, which means it can include more metadata than the relatively limited set that is stored in the candidate pool. The queue table tracks each volume's priority level, who added it, and where it came from.[73] The metadata also includes a

---

[73] Most volumes come to the queue from the candidate pool because their bibliographic metadata put them in-scope for copyright review, but some volumes are manually added in response to specific requests from patrons, or for some other reason.

Note that in the absence of other factors, volumes are added to the queue from those most recently added to the candidate pool. In other words, the pool is a LIFO stack ("last in, first out"). LIFO seemed appropriate because recently added volumes are more likely to be of immediate interest to someone.

TECHNICAL

locking mechanism to prevent a volume from being reviewed by more than one person at a time.

Both CRMS-US and CRMS-World have their own queue. Each night, overnight processing removes the volumes that have been reviewed that day and then replenishes each queue with enough candidates from its corresponding pool to bring the queue back up to its designated number of volumes.

THE QUEUING ALGORITHM

This is the bulk of the query used to select a volume for a normal (nonexpert) user to review. Some details related to subprojects have been omitted. If subprojects are present in the system, then the algorithm will further restrict the selection (e.g., AND q.project IN . . . or AND q.project NOT IN . . . based on whether the user is assigned to a subproject or not).

The query selects volumes that

- are of appropriate priority (level 1 is typically used for re-review projects, and anything 3 or higher is only available to experts or admins)
- are not locked
- have not had a status of 3 or higher set by overnight processing
- have not been reviewed already by the current reviewer
- have not in the past been reviewed by the current reviewer
- have only zero or one review

These results are sorted by priority first, then by number of reviews already done. The SHA2 hash is used to pseudorandomize the results so that two reviewers are less likely to try to select the same volume for review and possibly precipitate a race condition. The final ORDER BY clause—by time stamp—preserves some (or arguably none, given the SHA2 ordering) of the queue's LIFO character. The first volume in the result set that the user can successfully lock (i.e., set q.locked to *userid*) is the volume that CRMS presents for review.

In the listing below, instances of *userid* can be understood as the reviewer's CRMS id (e-mail address or Michigan uniqname). In practice, they would be wildcards against SQL injection attack and passed as parameters to the DBI module.

TECHNICAL

```
SELECT q.id,(SELECT COUNT(*) FROM reviews r WHERE
   r.id=q.id) AS cnt, SHA2(CONCAT(userid,q.id),0)
   as hash, q.priority FROM queue q
WHERE q.priority<3
AND q.priority!=1
AND q.locked IS NULL
AND q.status<2
AND NOT EXISTS (SELECT * FROM reviews r2 WHERE r2
   .id=q.id AND r2.user=userid)
AND NOT EXISTS (SELECT * FROM historicalreviews h
   WHERE h.id=q.id AND h.user=userid)
HAVING cnt<2
ORDER BY q.priority DESC, cnt DESC, hash, q.time
   ASC
```

The HathiTrust PageTurner Access and Authentication Modules

In order for a reviewer to do her work, that reviewer must be authorized to view in-copyright works in HathiTrust.

Four access and authentication modules in the HathiTrust PageTurner program perform this security function. The modules check the reviewer's profile and confirm that the reviewer is permitted to see copyrighted material for the purposes of copyright research. If the reviewer does not have that permission, PageTurner will refuse access to that reviewer and display only a message that the reviewer is not allowed to view copyrighted content. Unless that reviewer's permissions are changed, she will not be able to see in-copyright material.[74]

Access to in-copyright material is strictly enforced in CRMS. Reviewers must complete and submit a form called "Statement for Access to In-Copyright Works in HathiTrust" before they will be authorized for participation in CRMS.

---

[74] For more details about PageTurner and how HathiTrust protects access to copyrighted material, see HathiTrust, "Access Determination for HathiTrust Objects," accessed January 20, 2016, http://www.hathitrust.org/access_determination.

Statement for Access to In-Copyright Works in HathiTrust

By signing this Statement, I understand that I am being granted special access to in-copyright works in HathiTrust for one of the purposes below (please place an "X" next to the desired purposes):

	1. To create replacement copies of individual pages of volumes in HathiTrust.
	2. To evaluate the quality of digital volumes in HathiTrust, for purposes including digitization planning or evaluation as potential replacements for damaged print volumes.
	3. To perform in-print status review of volumes in HathiTrust.
	4. In support of corrections or updates to HathiTrust volumes (e.g., for the User Support Working Group).
	5. To correct or add information to the bibliographic records of volumes deposited in HathiTrust by my institution.
	6. To perform copyright review on HathiTrust volumes
	7. To operate or maintain HathiTrust repository infrastructure
	8. To develop software for HathiTrust services or operations

I understand that I may only use my special access for the purposes defined above. I agree to notify the University of Michigan (hathitrust-info@umich.edu) immediately if:

- I have any suspicion that in-copyright works are being used for purposes other than those specified above, or unauthorized access to in-copyright works has occurred.
- I have any questions or concerns about the uses I might make of volumes I access in the course of my work, or about the security of the workstation I am accessing from.
- My job responsibilities change and I should no longer have special access to in-copyright works in HathiTrust.

I understand that access is granted to me for the following period **12/1/2014 - 6/30/2015**. After this time access may be renewed with appropriate authorization. Authorization must be given by the same individual who approved access, or an individual of similar standing at the institution. Authorization should be sent to hathitrust-info@umich.edu.

By my signature, I certify that I have read the security requirements available at http://tinyurl.com/m59dmb6 and agree, working with appropriate systems staff if necessary, to ensure that my workstation is in compliance with the requirements during the time that I have special access to in-copyright works in HathiTrust.

Enter additional rows for staff as necessary:

Staff member name:	Signature:	Date:
Email:	Phone:	IP address:

For internal use:

Institutional approval granted by:
Authorization granted by:

Figure 13 Statement for Access form

TECHNICAL

THE REVIEW PROCESS

Once the reviewer is confirmed for access to in-copyright works, the review process can begin. There are several tools to help guide reviewers through the process; the most significant is the CRMS interface.

The reviewer must be logged into the CRMS interface and have her browser pointed to its "review" pane in order to see the scanned image of the volume under review. The interface provides relevant catalog information and review tools adjacent to the scan. A CRMS reviewer may review as much or as little of the work as necessary to make an accurate copyright determination, but in most cases the front matter of the volume (from title page to table of contents) provides the most relevant copyright-related information.

Each version of CRMS (-US, -World) has an associated decision tree, as do subprojects such as CRMS-Spain. Each decision tree lays out the research process as a step-by-step flowchart. This approach ensures that the reviewer considers every relevant factor and does so in a specific order. For a determination to be complete in CRMS, the reviewers must come to a compatible decision about a work ("pd," "pdus," "ic," "icus," or "und"). If two reviewers come to incompatible decisions, then their reviews are "in conflict," requiring an expert to adjudicate between them.

MISSING PAGES AND WRONG RECORDS

There is only one way that a volume in the queue can be removed from the system without receiving an exportable, final determination. This happens when either reviewer decides the volume cannot be determined because the scan is incomplete or because there is a mismatch between the scan and its associated bibliographic metadata.

First the reviewer will need to provide feedback about the problem to HathiTrust using a reporting tool in PageTurner. The review page displays a JavaScript alert when such a review is submitted, as a reminder that HathiTrust feedback is expected. (Due to cross-site security limitations, CRMS cannot detect whether or not the user has actually done so.)

Once the reviewer submits a review of a work with missing pages or a wrong record, the volume will be immediately removed from the review process (even though it may only have one review at that point). This prevents another reviewer from working on a scan that may not be complete or accurate.

If the volume still falls within the scope of CRMS review, a corrected scan can be moved to the appropriate queue at some time in the future.

System Response to Matches and Conflicts

Once two reviewers have submitted their judgments, the system checks for conflicts between the two reviews and responds accordingly. The system does this through the use of status codes.

TECHNICAL

STATUS CODES

The status codes described here are assigned during overnight processing, with the results showing in the system the following day. The exceptions to this are Status 5 and Status 6, which take place immediately. The note categories of "missing" or "wrong record" will be immediately assigned a Status 6. Any status higher than a Status 3 counts as a final determination.

Conflicts (Status 2)   If the two reviewers disagree, either about the attribute or about the reason, then the volume will move to Status 2 and be added to the "conflicts page" in the interface.

Over the years, we have made several modifications to the algorithms that classify each volume's pair of reviews based on whether they agree or disagree. In particular, we try to avoid requiring a full expert adjudication in cases where two reviews do not exactly match but would still have the same result (opening a volume or keeping it closed).

For example, in CRMS-US, copyright renewal numbers are not required to match because, by definition, the fact that there is a notice of renewal on a volume published between 1923 and 1963 means that volume will remain closed.

If the reviewers agree that the attribute should be ic, icus, or und, but then disagree about which reason should apply, then the volume will *not* move to Status 2 and be added to the conflicts page.[75] Because the final result will be that the volume will remain closed, refining the specific reason for the closure is not an effective use of time. This means that volumes in the conflicts page will always have at least one review that recommends either pd or pdus.

Provisional Matches (Status 3)   All work done by nonadvanced reviewers who have only recently completed their training is automatically assigned a Status 3 and added to a "provisional match" page where an expert can confirm it. The reviewer versus advanced reviewer distinction provides a period for new reviewers to demonstrate their consistent and reliable understanding of the process. Status 3 is also used for minor (typically author death date) mismatches between advanced reviewers that are not important enough to be considered Status 2 conflicts. (However, even this step will be skipped if both advanced reviewers have selected und/nfi.)

Matches (Status 4)   If the two reviewers agree—if both reviewers select the same rights (a.k.a. attribute) and the same reason—then the volume will move to Status 4 and be included in the export process that evening.

---

75 So ic and und are considered a "good enough" match in this case, and the determination is allowed to resolve to und/crms.

Expert Adjudication

Two reviews will typically be sufficient for an exportable copyright determination. In some cases, however, an expert will need to intervene in a conflict or a provisional match.

Experts can access conflicts and provisional match pages in the CRMS interface from a drop-down menu. Each page contains a list with each row representing one review of a volume (a typical volume will have two rows until an expert makes an adjudication). The lists make it easy for an expert to see at a glance all the review work done on a volume.

Each row also includes a link to the scan so the expert can access it and get a better understanding of how the reviewer reached that judgment. This takes place within a review interface that features radio buttons to allow the expert to toggle back and forth between the two reviews. When the expert is ready to make an adjudication, the modified interface will also allow her to import a preferred review's data and notes into her own review, saving her some keystrokes and allowing her to add comments to the previous work.

TECHNICAL

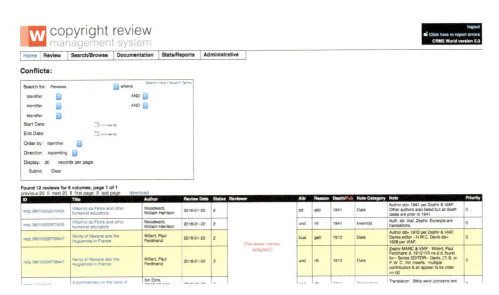

Figure 16 Conflicts table

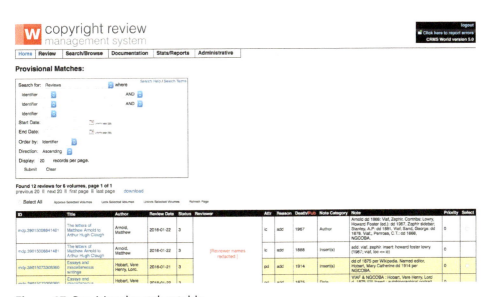

Figure 17 Provisional matches table

The expert examines the conflicting reviews and other data pertaining to that volume, adds comments or corrections as necessary, and then submits her own review. The expert's judgment will be exported to the HathiTrust Rights Database that evening, except in cases where an und/nfi determination would inappropriately prevent US access.

GROUP IDS AND RE-REVIEWS

Upon completion, the expert review will be assigned a group ID. All the reviews made on a given volume are assigned the same "group ID" (gid) in the CRMS system. If that volume is later selected for re-review (for whatever reason) and put through the CRMS review process again, then there will be a new set of reviews on it, and these will be assigned a different gid. Therefore a volume will have as many associated gids as the number of times it has gone through the CRMS review process. The gid is implemented as an auto-incrementing number in the "determinations" table.

Overnight Processing

That evening, the overnight processing script responds to the work done that day.

First, Status 0 volumes with two reviews are moved to Status 2, 3, or 4, depending on whether they are a conflict, provisional, or match.

TECHNICAL

Next, Status 4 (or higher) volumes are moved from the reviews table to historical reviews (indicating they have completed the review process) and the determinations table. Determinations eligible for export are written to a text file for the Rights Database to read.

> The determinations table is similar to the queue table but includes the volume's final determination (including attribute and reason) and a flag to indicate if the determination was exported to the Rights Database. Determinations are to historical reviews as the queue is to reviews. The determinations table preserves the various tracking fields found in the queue. It also assigns a group ID that explicitly links it to the historical reviews that contributed to the determination.

Overnight processing also updates user statistics, including monthly review counts and validation numbers, and updates export statistics. Finally, overnight processing replenishes the queue to a predetermined amount greater than the number of reviews that can be completed in one day.

Inheritance

The overnight processing phase "export inheritance" takes each volume that has been added to the determinations table in the last twenty-four hours and identifies all the other volumes associated with its catalog ID. These copies now become inheriting volumes and will inherit the same determinations as their corresponding source volumes (the specific scanned copies that actually went through the CRMS review process).

Here is an example of export inheritance: A volume—for instance, an edition of *Kwaidan* by Lafcadio Hearn from 1907—receives two reviews (both of them in complete agreement). That evening, overnight processing checks the corresponding HathiTrust catalog record and finds another copy of that edition of *Kwaidan* (not yet reviewed by CRMS) associated with that record. This other volume now becomes an "inheriting volume" and inherits the same rights determination as the first volume.

"Candidates inheritance" is a mirror process to "export inheritance" that addresses the opposite situation. The former matches a source with inheriting volumes, while the latter matches a new inheriting volume with an old source.

For example, three months have passed since the export inheritance example above, and a new institution joins the HathiTrust community with a copy of the same edition of *Kwaidan* in its library. "Candidates inheritance" checks the new volume and discovers it to be a match for the same catalog record as the earlier two copies of *Kwaidan*. The process identifies the new copy as an inheriting volume, automatically generates a determination for it, and then exports that determination to the HathiTrust Rights Database.

INHERITANCE

The core of this algorithm takes a determination, with proposed source and inheriting volumes, and determines the reason, if any, for the inheritance not to take place. Inheritance is disallowed when any one of the following is true:

- The catalog record has enum/chron information for any volume on it.
- There is a newer determination for any other volume on the record.
- Current rights for the inheriting volume cannot be determined (due to a database connectivity issue).
- The inherited determination is pd/ncn ("no copyright notice" on the logic that the notice may be absent due to missing pages).

Once an inheriting volume passes the above tests, one or more of the following must be true of the inheriting volume's current rights in order for inheritance to take place:

- Rights are in CRMS scope ("CRMS-exportable" rights).
- Rights are pdus/gfv and the determination is pd or pdus.
- Rights are ic/bib.
- Rights are pdus (CRMS-World only).

Approved inheritances are subsequently divided into two groups: (1) those that have had a prior expert's determination in CRMS, and (2) those that have not. An expert must approve items in the first group; determinations from the second group are handled automatically as part of overnight processing. A successful inheritance is typically submitted to the Rights Database a day after the inheritance algorithm approves it, allowing administrators a window to review and potentially delete those that may be problematic. (To our knowledge, this has never happened; it was insurance against unanticipated problems in the early days after the inheritance feature was deployed.)

CRMS Exports and the HathiTrust Rights Database

At this point, the work of CRMS is done except for exporting the determination to the Rights Database.

CRMS sends its determinations to HathiTrust in the form of a text file, and HathiTrust uses these determinations to update the volumes' rights information in the HathiTrust Rights Database.

Rejections of CRMS determinations are exceptionally rare, though they do happen—usually when HathiTrust has information that was not available to CRMS reviewers at the time reviewers made a given determination.

CAN THIS DETERMINATION BE EXPORTED?

This algorithm is applied during an overnight process to determine whether a determination should be written to the file that is imported into the HathiTrust Rights Database. Regardless of the outcome, the determination is always stored in the CRMS database.

The purpose of this algorithm was originally to prevent und/* determinations in CRMS-World from closing volumes that are pdus/bib. It was expanded to cover Status 6 when that was introduced, and to cover certain other edge cases, many of which are rather unlikely. (We err on the side of caution: better to fail to export an appropriate determination and catch it later than to export an inappropriate determination.)

A determination is ineligible for export if any of the following conditions hold:

- The determination is a Status 6 (missing pages/wrong record).
- The system variable noExport is set and the queue priority is less than 3.
- The current rights for the volume make it out of scope, unless any one of the following is true:
  - Current rights are pdus/gfv.
  - Priority is 3 or greater.
  - Current rights were submitted by a CRMS system (US/World).
  - Determination is pd.
  - Determination is pdus and current rights are not pd.

TECHNICAL

Pilot Projects

This section gives brief overviews of several pilot projects we did in the course of executing the suite of CRMS projects. Several opportunities arose to experiment with a variety of applications of the CRMS model. There is considerable interest in this work and in how it may be extensible to works from other countries, subject to the laws of other nations, and other media beyond books.

We experimented with books from Spain in HathiTrust as a formal part of our second grant from the IMLS in conjunction with the Universidad Complutense de Madrid. Opportunities arose throughout the CRMS projects that allowed us to test theories and improve resources, from reviewing books from Spain with scans in the CRMS interface to reviewing Spanish-language books without scans. We also tested reviewing books from Germany and adapted the CRMS interface to develop versions of CRMS that could be used for future projects. Other work included improvement of Name Authority Cooperative Program (NACO) records and review of government documents produced by US states, which are presumptively subject to copyright, unlike the work of employees of the US federal government.

REVIEWING WORKS PUBLISHED IN SPAIN

Collaborators: Dean Atiya, Antonio Moreno Cañizares, Nerea Llamas, Almudena Caballos Villar

PILOT PROJECTS

CRMS developed a pilot program to review a limited set of Spanish-language volumes published in Spain. The pilot built on research performed by HathiTrust partner Universidad Complutense de Madrid.

KEY OBSERVATIONS

- Preliminary research on author death dates will allow you to refine your candidate pool by eliminating authors whose works are still in copyright. This allows your project to focus resources on reviewing works likely to be in the public domain.
- Just two or three reviewers can reasonably review a candidate pool with fewer than a thousand volumes. The corresponding investment in startup and training time will be better balanced with the amount of work.
- Foreign language and more complex works benefit from a team empowered to both reference a decision tree and apply reasoned judgment in new situations.
- An author-based approach—reviewing works by the same author in succession—is particularly advantageous with a pool containing multiple works by the same author.

Introduction

In collaboration with Universidad Complutense de Madrid, HathiTrust's first partner outside the United States, we piloted a project to review Spanish-language books published in Spain. Complutense was

PILOT PROJECTS

interested in a significant number of scans of the books from their collection; they wanted to make these available for annotation. The books had not yet been reviewed for copyright status and were thus inaccessible to users in Spain. Specifically, the Complutense researchers prepared a list of Spanish author names and death dates to inform the scope of our inquiry. Complutense approached HathiTrust with a proposal for collaboration with LEETHI (Literaturas Españolas y Europeas del Texto al Hipermedia) and ILSA (Implementation of Language-Driven Software and Applications) research groups. Their project, "Mnemosine: The Digital Library of Rare and Forgotten Spanish Texts (1868–1939)," centered on building a system for annotating public domain digital texts. Our review of HathiTrust volumes facilitated this project.[76]

Project Design

The project was designed to review Spanish-language works through a modification to the CRMS-World infrastructure. The interface was adapted based on Spanish copyright law.

Candidate pool
- Approximately seven hundred volumes
- Works first published in Spain

---

76 For more information related to these projects, see Complutense, Grupo de Investigación, "Grupo de Investigación L.E.E.T.H.I. (Literaturas Españolas y Europeas del Texto al Hipermedia)," accessed January 20, 2016, https://www.ucm.es/leethi.

- Primary author death dates preconfirmed to be 1934 and earlier
- Monographic works only

Time frame
- CRMS interface modifications—one week developer time
- Legal research and project preplanning—two to three weeks
- Review of seven hundred volumes—approximately one month

Staffing
- Copyright research specialist
- Three reviewers familiar with Romance languages
- Project manager and developer

Desired outcomes
- Open volumes
- Collect data on efficacy of using an author-centered approach
- Gain experience in assessing foreign language front matter (publication conventions, terminology, inserts)

Funding
- All activity supported through CRMS grant funds and allocation of cost-share time

Workflow

We created a partition within the CRMS-World interface as a low-cost way of performing Spanish-language reviews without committing to

PILOT PROJECTS

the development of a stand-alone interface solely for Spanish publications. This allowed us to proceed quickly with only minor software development.

From a spreadsheet of Spanish authors provided by Universidad Complutense de Madrid, we selected only authors with a confirmed death date prior to 1934. Given the Spanish copyright term of author life + 80 years, we decided that any monograph with a primary author death date of 1934 or later was not an eligible candidate. The list of eligible authors was matched against bibliographic records in HathiTrust to create a candidate pool of volumes; often there would be several volumes per author.

The copyright specialist performed a preliminary test of our review process with a limited number of volumes. This check did not identify any unforeseen issues with the candidates, so we went ahead with the CRMS double-review process, following the decision tree below:

PILOT PROJECTS

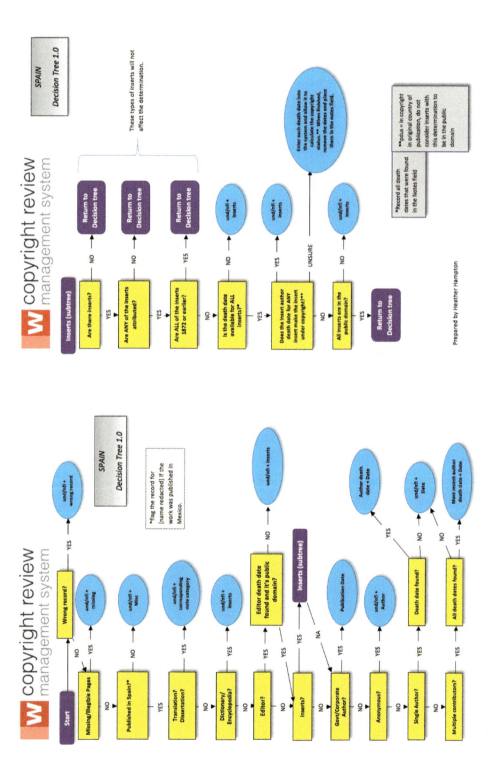

Figures 18 & 19 Decision tree for reviewing works published in Spain

PILOT PROJECTS

INTERFACE PARTITION DEVELOPMENT

This pilot prompted a modification of the queuing mechanism that allowed us to selectively assign works to specific reviewers on a project. We feel this kind of queue partitioning has turned out to be a valuable tool for managing and implementing separate projects.

Final Observations

1. A concern at the outset of this project was that reviewers would need to be fluent in Spanish. We discovered, however, that a moderate familiarity with Romance languages was sufficient. Publishing conventions and similarities in front matter, combined with online translation tools, provided enough context to analyze copyright-relevant information.
2. The resources most accessible to non-Spanish speakers were the Virtual International Authority File (VIAF) and Spanish Wikipedia. Language was a barrier to searching foreign language databases such as Spanish newspaper archives for author death dates. Collaboration with language specialists may help expand the scope of a copyright review project. The native speakers from Universidad Complutense de Madrid provided us with author death dates from sources such as the *El País* newspaper, which we would not have been able to find on our own.
3. We saw greater efficiency when works by the same author were reviewed in close proximity. A number of authors tended to publish greatly similar works with repetitive use of coauthors, editors, and illustrators. Reviewing these works in succession made it easier to recall dates and sources without repeating a recently completed search.
4. An author-based research process, in which a reviewer's confirmation of an author's death date and nationality could then be

propagated to other works by that author, would be more efficient for copyright regimes based on the life of the author.
5. Over the course of the project, we identified information gaps, which specialists more familiar with Spanish works could have helped us resolve. (Developing a mechanism for soliciting help from a specialist community is ideal.)
6. Reviews for this pool of candidates required 56 hours. Approximately 20 hours of developer time was needed to set up the infrastructure. Average review time per volume was 18.9 minutes.

Outcomes

In total, we reviewed 730 volumes, 467 of which were determined to be in the public domain.

The primary reasons for keeping a work closed were as follows:

1. The volume was coauthored by an author who died after 1934.
2. We could not locate a coauthor's death date.
3. The volume included in-copyright or unknown copyright photographs, paintings, and other works created by third parties.

PILOT PROJECTS

LATIN AMERICAN WORKS FROM THE BENSON COLLECTION AT UNIVERSITY OF TEXAS AT AUSTIN

This scenario describes a pilot project of Spanish-language works carried out by the University of Texas at Austin (UT). This pilot was carried out using physical volumes rather than the CRMS interface because of contractual restrictions placed on UT's scans. The information in this report was taken from the presentation "CRMS South America: A Study of Argentine Monographs in the Benson Latin American Collection, University of Texas at Austin," presented by Carlos Ovalle, Caron Garstka, and Georgia Harper in September 2014 to the CRMS Advisory Working Group.

KEY OBSERVATIONS

- Digital scans are essential to performing copyright determinations at a large scale.
- A structured process may be reliably performed by graduate students under supervision.
- A mechanism to predict entry into the public domain should be considered when gathering copyright duration–relevant data.

PILOT PROJECTS

Introduction

This pilot was conceived and run by Georgia K. Harper, a member of the CRMS Advisory Working Group and Scholarly Communications Advisor at University of Texas at Austin Libraries. She engaged the help of Carlos Ovalle and Caron Garstka, two graduate students from the UT School of Information. The project centered around the Benson Latin American Collection, a valuable resource of UT Libraries that contains materials on Mexico, Central and South America, the Caribbean, and the Hispanic presence in the United States.

Most volumes in the Benson collection were digitized, but at the time of this inquiry, it was not possible to obtain access to the digital scans of in-copyright works. This pilot was designed to evaluate the efficacy of reviewing physical books for the purpose of copyright review using the CRMS methodology without the interface tool.

Libraries sometimes approach us to find out how to use CRMS to make copyright determinations on yet unscanned works in analog form with the aspiration of identifying only public domain works that would in turn be candidates for scanning. This is feasible but terrifically inefficient without the benefits of robust documentation.

PILOT PROJECTS

Project Design

The project was modeled after CRMS, including two independent reviews of each volume and a narrow project scope. Lack of access to digital scans meant that the project could not employ the CRMS online interface. Data collection was by spreadsheet.

Candidate pool
- Sample of one hundred volumes
- Argentinian published monographs
- Publication dates ranging primarily from 1906 to 2005
- Because of the nature of the collection, 88 percent were published post 1940
- Selected randomly, but selected volumes represented one hundred unique authors

Time frame
- Five-month timeline
  - Four months for library staff to create the book list because of problems with system software migration
  - One week for library staff to pull the books from shelf; ten books could be pulled per hour, provided the books were on site
  - Sixteen to twenty hours for researchers to enter catalog data
  - Eight to sixteen hours for researchers to determine author death dates

PILOT PROJECTS

Staffing
- Scholarly Communications Advisor at UT
- Two UT graduate students with Spanish comprehension

Desired outcomes
- Develop proof of concept for comprehensive rights review by UT
- Collect data
  - Ascertain time and labor required for completion of entire pool
  - Conceptualize a longer term project
- Predict future entry into the public domain of currently copyrighted works
- Assess whether CRMS assumptions about inserts were significant and their implications for determining public domain status of a work otherwise believed to be in the public domain
- Have a basis to determine whether "principal text in the public domain" should be a rights category for allowing access to digital scans

Funding
- All activity funded internally by UT

Other factors that aided in this pilot were
- access to Benson collection curators
- access to a library cataloger for general cataloging questions
- working knowledge of written Spanish
- Google Translate

PILOT PROJECTS

Workflow

The University of Michigan CRMS team supplied informative resources, both legal and procedural, to assist UT in setting up their workflow. The UT researchers selected a set of a hundred Argentinian monographs from the Benson collection for copyright review. Because the digital scans had not been deposited in HathiTrust, the rights metadata could not be collected in the standard CRMS fashion and thereby associated with a unique volume. Therefore, UT developed their own data collection procedure, modeling it on the data collected by CRMS. Lack of access to digital scans also necessitated a revised workflow to accommodate working with physical volumes.

According to the legal research done by UT, Argentine copyright law requires registration. Verifying registration would have been very costly and impractical to implement in the workflow, so UT began with a presumption of registration for their entire sample because registration could potentially occur at any time prior to copyright expiration. UT's legal research also indicated that in the case of translations, authorization was required for up to ten years after the death of the author. After this time, anyone could make a translation without authorization by paying an arbitrated fee. They found that whether a translation was authorized was not always clear. This has an impact on the rights a translator could hold in the translation.

UT student researchers identified at least one reliable source for each author death date—preferably two sources in accordance with

CRMS-World standards. Two people at UT independently reviewed each volume and then examined the results jointly. Useful Argentinian author death date resources included the UT catalog, Biblioteca del Congreso, Wikipedia, LoC Name Authorities, Google Search, social media such as LinkedIn, university websites, newspaper articles, Biografias y Vidas, Minibiografias, and Todotango.com.

Final Observations

1. Digital scans are essential to a viable process for copyright review. Selecting a sample from the Benson collection and then pulling volumes from the shelves was prohibitively time and labor intensive. Any large-scale review system would necessarily depend on the availability of scanned content.
2. Future projects may seek ways to engage graduate students as reviewers. Features of a program involving graduate students should include a monitored, consistent process applied to all reviewed works and minimal judgment required once a framework has been established.
3. Foreign language volumes raise specific issues related to the characteristics of the language. For example, accented characters proved to be a complicating factor for searching the catalog record.
4. Due to a sample set that was predominantly composed of late twentieth-century volumes, many of the works in the Argentine collection will not enter the public domain for many years. However, a long-term strength of this pilot was the collection of

relevant metadata to assist in determining when a work would enter the public domain in the future. UT recommended including a "predicted public domain" date within the CRMS system, with a mechanism for flagging works entering the public domain at the beginning of each year.
5. Storage changes to the collection over time had an impact on how accessible the physical volumes were for this pilot.

Outcomes

One hundred volumes were reviewed; the project results are as follows:

Undetermined—needing further investigation
- 64 percent of volumes had inserts
- 16 percent of volumes were compilations with many authors
- 3 percent were translations

Reliability assessment
- One instance of a differing death date between independent reviews
- One instance of locating an author with two death dates
- Catalog information was 99 percent accurate in terms of author information
    - One entry mentioned two authors but only one author could be found within the work
    - Catalog data often indicated "et al." for multiple author entries rather than listing all names

PILOT PROJECTS

Found to be public domain
- Nine public domain in Argentina
- Eight public domain in the United States
- Four public domain in both Argentina and the United States

Volumes able to forecast a date of copyright expiration
- Thirty-one predicted with copyright expiration date in Argentina
- Forty-six predicted with copyright expiration date in the United States
- Thirty-one predicted with copyright expiration date in both Argentina and the United States

Results: Author information identified
- Thirty-nine authors were identified as probably still living
- Thirty-seven authors had definitive death dates
- Fifteen authors could not be found
- Three items were authored by a government or entity without individual personal attribution

HUMBOLDT UNIVERSITY OF BERLIN: RIGHTS RESEARCH PROJECT FOR GERMAN BOOKS

Collaborators: Lovis Atze, Rebecca Behnk, Karina Georgi, Regine Granzoq, Joyce Ray, Michael Seadle

PILOT PROJECTS

This scenario describes a pilot project of German editions of Greek and Latin classical texts carried out by iSchool students at Humboldt-Universität zu Berlin. In this project, we were unable to provide access to scans for the purposes of copyright review; physical volumes were pulled from the Humboldt Library collection for examination.

KEY OBSERVATIONS

- Copyright review using physical books from another library required careful comparison with catalog records of the digital scan to ensure an exact match of volumes and editions.
- VIAF was the most useful resource, even when compared to resources specifically about German authors.
- Students with no previous experience in copyright were exposed to copyright concepts and able to learn and perform copyright review within the time span of a university term.

Introduction

Over half a million books in HathiTrust are published in German, which is the second most represented language in the collection after English. This indicates a rich source of books about art, science, medicine, and classics—all prominent areas of German scholarship and heavily represented in North American research libraries. We speculate that some of these may no longer exist in Germany because of the disruption of war. If identified as public domain, these could be made widely available.

PILOT PROJECTS

Project Design

This project was initiated by Michael Seadle, a Director and Dean at the Institut für Bibliotheks- und Informationswissenschaft (IBI) at Humboldt and led by visiting professor Joyce Ray, Program Coordinator and Lecturer for the Johns Hopkins University Museum Studies program.

Graduate students enrolled in the IBI summer project seminar learned how to make copyright determinations on German works. Legal assumptions were formulated with collaboration from Katharina de la Durantaye, Juniorprofessur für Bürgerliches Recht, insbesondere Internationales Privatrecht und Rechtsvergleichung, Humboldt-Universität zu Berlin. The class met with Melissa Levine via Skype under Professor Ray's direction.

Candidate pool
- Approximately 120 volumes
- German monographic works from a HathiTrust collection entitled "German editions of Greek and Latin Works 1873–1933"
- Works were by ancient authors, with additive content by more contemporary German editors

Time frame
- Three months, during the IBI summer term

Staffing
- Four students enrolled in the IBI project seminar

PILOT PROJECTS

Desired outcomes
- Serve as a learning exercise for IBI students; results were not intended to be legally actionable for HathiTrust
- Identify impediments, legal and practical, to operating a collaborative rights review of German works with an international partner
- Evaluate processes and resources for performing copyright determination on works of German authorship

Funding
- All activity funded internally by Humboldt University or part of seminar requirements for the students

Workflow

With the help of experts in German law, the students learned about copyright as it relates to German authors' rights and copyright term. They compiled a list of works to be examined, created a spreadsheet of editor names extracted from those works, and identified reliable resources in which to search for death date information. The students opted to take a name-based approach by assigning each editor a unique number and searching once for all works by that editor in the candidate pool. At least two students searched each editor's name to confirm dates in multiple sources.

In order to confirm that the works researched by students and those in HathiTrust were the same, the students photocopied the front matter of each work and submitted it to staff at the University of Michigan for verification prior to applying a rights determination to the digital scan. Upon verification that the rights determinations had been performed upon matching volumes, HathiTrust then opened up the books that students identified as being public domain in Germany.

As part of the IBI coursework, students kept a record of their search process and noted their observations of the usefulness of various death date sources. Their experiences are published in a D-Lib paper, "Testing the HathiTrust Copyright Search Protocol in Germany: A Pilot Project on Procedures and Resources," *D-Lib Magazine* 20, no. 9/10.

Final Observations

1. For foreign language works, the compilation of a glossary of terms and abbreviations was helpful. The students translated words and phrases most helpful when searching for and interpreting terminology used in the front matter of a work.
2. Bibliographic metadata containing author and editor death dates immensely simplified the copyright review process. Of fifty authors represented in the sample set, only twelve required a death date search. Of those twelve, despite a detailed search being performed, some editor death dates were not findable (although rough "flourished" dates could be inferred). Perhaps some copyright determinations could be based on knowledge of life-spans and living dates even when a precise death date cannot be found.

PILOT PROJECTS

3. Students realized that volumes could have multiple entries in HathiTrust when different schools had contributed a scan of the same volume. They needed to make sure that only one copyright determination was performed when the result could be applied to multiple copies of the same work in HathiTrust.
4. As in other CRMS projects, the top two sources for death date information continued to be a work's catalog record and the VIAF, even when the project is based on non-English works.
5. Students attempted without success to gain access to databases and records kept by German publisher Teubner-Verlag, the Deutsches Historisches Museum, and VG Wort, a collecting society for German authors and publishers. It is unknown whether having access to those records would have impacted the outcome for editors whose death dates could not be discovered, but it highlighted the importance of having open resources to aid copyright determination projects.

Outcomes

The student project resulted in the following outcomes:

- Students identified author and editor death dates for 109 volumes.
- Students identified one hundred volumes as public domain; these volumes were opened in HathiTrust.
- Students identified nine volumes as in copyright; these volumes remained closed in HathiTrust.

- Students prepared a glossary of German/English publishing terms to facilitate future research of German-language works.
- Students compiled a list of reputable death date sources for German authors and editors.[77]

CONTRIBUTING TO NAME AUTHORITY COOPERATIVE PROGRAM (NACO) RECORDS

CRMS developed a pilot program working with the Name Authority Cooperative Program (NACO) to enhance authority records during the CRMS-World grant period (2011–14).

---

77 Rebecca Behnk, Karina Georgi, Regine Granzow and Lovis Atze. "Testing the HathiTrust Copyright Search Protocol in Germany: A Pilot Project on Procedures and Resources," *D-Lib Magazine* 20, no. 9/10 (2014), doi:10.1045/september2014-behnk.

PILOT PROJECTS

KEY OBSERVATIONS

- NACO provides libraries with a mechanism to create or refine authority records in support of copyright determination.
- There is a shortage of NACO-trained catalogers and a backlog of work. Enhancing authority records with copyright-relevant information greatly increases the efficiency of copyright review. Libraries should continue to explore ways to contribute this data to discoverable and centralized repositories.
- Death date resources vary in quality. Contributions to NACO records centralize death dates in an authoritative and trusted online resource.

Introduction

Copyright review is most efficient when the catalog record contains an author's death date.[78] When a death date is absent, the reviewer must look to outside resources for this information. CRMS-World reviewers often identified author data that had not yet been added to name authority records. However, our systems were not able to update catalog records automatically, so author data captured for a single review would not be accessible for future reviews of that author's work.

---

78 This statement presumes the copyright determination is being made based on the death date of the author. In contrast, as with CRMS-US, copyright determinations may also be based on copyright formalities such as renewal and copyright notice.

PILOT PROJECTS

Post Mortem Auctoris (PMA) is how copyright term duration is calculated in the UK, Canada, and Australia. The arrival of a volume into the public domain is dependent on the author's death date. In many cases, copyright duration is not determined by the year of publication and conceptually all published works by an author come into public domain at the same time.

In order to address this issue, we created a pilot project in partnership with our library's NACO liaison to funnel author information back into NACO authority records, which are exported to VIAF each month. VIAF is a primary source for finding author death dates; it receives data from national libraries around the world. The standards national libraries have established for creating name authority records are long-standing and trustworthy. Consequently, VIAF has proven to be the most central and reliable source for author death dates that is currently available on the open web.

We offer details about this pilot project below in the hope that future copyright review projects will also contribute to this important work.

Project Design

The project was designed to engage the problem in a low-tech, low-cost way. The following parameters informed the design of this project:

Intent
- Improve copyright-relevant data by contributing research to authority records
- Raise awareness nationally on the value of enhancing authority records for copyright determination
- As the project progressed, a new goal emerged to explore ways for expanding the activity to additional HathiTrust institutions

PILOT PROJECTS

Time frame
- Began in 2013 and continued for the duration of the CRMS grant

Staffing and volunteers
- Four CRMS reviewers contribute monthly spreadsheets
- Two U-M Technical Services catalogers update RDA NACO authority records
- Volunteer catalogers at Northwestern University, University of Chicago, and University of Minnesota

Funding
- Reviewer time is allocated as part of their CRMS grant cost-share contribution
- U-M Technical Services time is allocated as part of salaried work time

Workflow

We started the pilot project with a small group of catalogers certified to meet RDA NACO standards. A few CRMS reviewers who were interested in contributing to this pilot volunteered to collect author death dates as they performed reviews. These reviewers maintained a spreadsheet with death dates identified during the course of their work. At the end of each month, the reviewers e-mailed the spreadsheet to the U-M Technical

PILOT PROJECTS

Services Division. An RDA NACO cataloger then worked through the spreadsheet to update or create NACO name authority records.[79]

On average, seventy-five death dates are collected each month and it takes an estimated fifteen minutes to update one authority record. Each cataloger regularly contributes no less than two hours per week, with the following workflow:

The NACO trained cataloger searches the Library of Congress Name Authority File (LC NAF) through OCLC Connexion for possible variants of the name. If there is an existing authority record, they add the following:

- A closing death date to a preexisting birth date in the 100 field
- Birth and/or death dates to an 046 field
- A 370 subfield c location to designate the author's "associated place" (use established place headings, noting source in subfield 2)
- 670 fields to add citations that support the information we added; use subfield u to link to URLs as needed

They upgrade the record to RDA, if necessary, by

- changing the rules fixed field to z and adding rda to subfield e in the 040 field

---

[79] Caveat: Our NACO workflow is dependent on interaction with the CRMS grant and local U-M cataloging policies. Other institutions might choose to do this differently.

PILOT PROJECTS

- taking any other steps necessary to make sure that the record is fully RDA compliant

If the name does not have an existing authority record, the cataloger creates an authority record according to RDA rules and NACO and PCC guidelines, including death date and domicile/nationality (if available).

Catalogers are free to add additional information if available, such as other forms of a name in the 400 field. We are most concerned with the death date, associated place, and source documentation. Once the records are created or existing records are updated, they are sent to the NACO liaison for review and bibliographic file management.

Final Observations

1. Incorporate copyright-relevant information in cataloging practices. Cataloging practice does not require an author death date to be included in a record. Cataloging practice was not designed to serve copyright evaluation needs, and in many cases, the focus was on the creation of sufficient metadata for the disambiguation of content, not its complete description. With library budget cuts, catalogers may need reasons to justify spending time on what may be perceived by department managers as unnecessary information. On the contrary, this basic factual information is critical metadata today.
2. The majority of authors identified by this pilot did not have existing NACO authority records. This information gap is an area of

PILOT PROJECTS

opportunity for those who wish to assist with public domain determination. Some rich sources for death dates have been public domain books in HathiTrust and Google Books (e.g., published proceedings of professional societies with obituaries for members). Public domain material can be used to help discover information relevant to copyright determinations.

3. Rights and access issues are a primary concern for digital collection development. Enhancing authority records with optional fields does take time but also has a significant impact on our ability to identify public domain works. For books still in copyright, prediction tools can use author metadata to anticipate when works will enter the public domain.
4. The number of death dates generated by CRMS indicates the benefit of linking copyright review projects with bibliographic enhancement initiatives. However, any library with a NACO liaison can independently work on enhancing authority records. This activity does not need to be coordinated or centralized within a copyright review project like CRMS.

Outcomes

From August 2014 to July 2015, participants in the NACO project spent 143 hours resulting in 1,277 edits to an existing record or the creation of a new record. The average time per record was 14.9 minutes.

PILOT PROJECTS

US STATE GOVERNMENT DOCUMENTS

This scenario describes a smaller project within CRMS-US to review the copyright status of approximately 61,000 US state government documents.

KEY OBSERVATIONS

- There is a need for libraries and state agencies to work together and collaborate on scanning, preserving, and hosting state documents.
- On average, over 70 percent of candidates in our project were found to have entered the public domain based on absence of copyright notice.
- At this time, public domain determinations have been the most efficient means of making state government documents available. It can be difficult to identify state officials with authority to grant permission, and most states lack policy in this area.

Introduction

When initially studying the question of state government documents in HathiTrust, we explored securing permission from authorized state representatives. We also looked for states that, through legislation, had explicitly dedicated government documents to the public domain. These lines of inquiry were inconclusive, and we shifted our focus to what could be accomplished through copyright review. We have found copyright review of state government documents to be straightforward, with few complications and a high likelihood of works found to be in the public domain.

Project Design

The workflow for reviewing state government documents easily mapped onto the CRMS-US infrastructure, allowing us to avoid the costs of a new project design.

These are the parameters informing the design of this project. All work was based on existing CRMS-US infrastructure and workflow modified for US state documents.

Candidate pool
- Approximately 61,000 volumes
- First publication in United States with publication dates between 1923 and 1977 (Hawaii and Alaska limited to items published from 1960 to 1977)
- State government documents only

Time frame
- Work to continue for the duration of the CRMS grant period
- Completion of entire pool of candidates is not expected

PILOT PROJECTS

Staffing
- Copyright research specialist
- Three reviewers with previous experience on the CRMS-US process
- Project manager and developer

Desired outcomes
- Open volumes full-text within the United States
- Collect data on the following:
  - Cases where copyright notice is present in US state government documents
  - Time and labor required for completion of entire pool
  - How often copyright notice is indicated in the back matter

Funding
- All activity supported through CRMS grant funds and allocation of cost-share time

PILOT PROJECTS

Workflow

We generated a candidate pool using standard bibliographic indicators for US state government documents. US copyright law required copyright notice through 1977, so that year became the outer boundary of our inquiry.[80]

We selected staff that were experienced with the CRMS-US decision tree and taught them the slight modifications required for reviewing US state documents. The project followed the standard CRMS double-review process using the decision tree below.

---

80 Technically, notice was a requirement of copyright through 1989, but lack of notice could be cured by registration after 1977. See Peter Hirtle, "Copyright Term and the Public Domain in the United States," last modified January 3, 2016, http://copyright.cornell.edu/resources/publicdomain.cfm.

PILOT PROJECTS

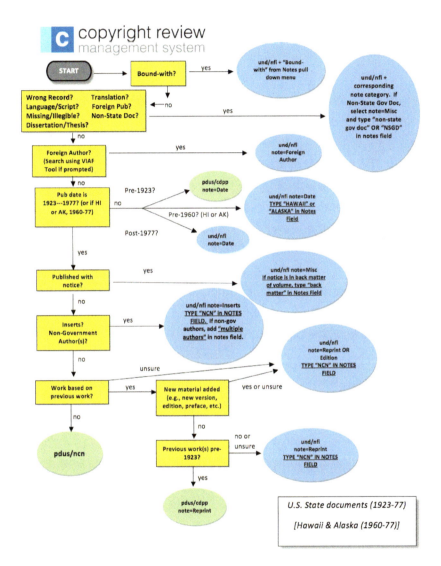

Figure 20 US state government document decision tree

During the process, reviewers confirmed that the work was in fact a state government document before focusing on three key elements:

1. The presence or absence of a copyright notice in the government document, including whether it appears in the back matter
2. Whether the work was a reprint of an earlier in-copyright work
3. Whether the work contained potentially in-copyright additional materials, such as a photograph produced by a third party

When a work did not contain third-party content, was not a reprint of an in-copyright work, and did not bear a copyright notice, it was determined to be in the US public domain.

Final Observations

1. Reviewing state government documents for a lack of copyright notice is a relatively simple workflow with a high probability of identifying volumes as in the public domain. Stats from the first five-month period showed that out of 5,527 reviews performed, 71.5 percent were found to be public domain. In comparison, the public domain average of the cumulative CRMS-US project was 51.7 percent.
2. A "bound-with" volume is one in which multiple, individually published documents have been bound together. Bound-withs present problems because they can require a lengthy process of checking internal sections of the volume for copyright notice. When one document bears a copyright notice, it

PILOT PROJECTS

will result in keeping the entire bound-with volume closed. We gave reviewers the option to disregard bound-withs due to their potential complexity. Our initial data collection showed that in 853 out of 17,307 reviews, the volume was determined to be a bound-with.
3. Copyright review based on publication with notice can potentially be applied to other types of US publications.

Outcomes

The project results, current as of March 2015, are as follows:

- 25,329 total reviews
- 9,846 exported determinations

BREAKDOWN OF RESULTS FOR US STATE GOVERNMENT DOCUMENT REVIEW (AS OF MARCH 2015)

Categories	May 2014	Jun 2014	Jul 2014	Aug 2014	Sep 2014	Oct 2014	Nov 2014	Dec 2014	Jan 2015	Feb 2015	Mar 2015
Public domain reviews	639 (62.6 percent)	1,107 (67.2 percent)	1,486 (75.5 percent)	781 (81.0 percent)	625 (75.6 percent)	734 (72.7 percent)	687 (71.0 percent)	450 (80.8 percent)	1,060 (71.2 percent)	1967 (70.9 percent)	2048 (67.1 percent)
In-copyright reviews	8 (0.8 percent)	88 (5.3 percent)	55 (2.8 percent)	7 (0.7 percent)	7 (0.8 percent)	3 (0.3 percent)	0 (0.0 percent)	0 (0.0 percent)	4 (0.3 percent)	16 (0.6 percent)	8 (0.3 percent)
Undetermined/ needs further investigation reviews	373 (36.6 percent)	452 (27.4 percent)	427 (21.7 percent)	176 (18.3 percent)	195 (23.6 percent)	272 (27.0 percent)	280 (29.0 percent)	107 (19.2 percent)	425 (28.5 percent)	792 (28.5 percent)	994 (32.6 percent)
Total reviews	1,020	1,647	1,968	964	827	1,009	967	557	1,489	2,775	3,050
Time per review (mins)	1.1	0.8	0.9	1.2	1.3	1.3	1.4	1.5	1.3	0.9	0.9

Appendices

This section provides additional insight into practical tools developed by CRMS. The materials below include CRMS decision trees, personnel job descriptions, and reviewer training materials. For more information and additional documentation, visit the CRMS project webpage at http://www.lib.umich.edu/imls-national-leadership-grant-crms-world.

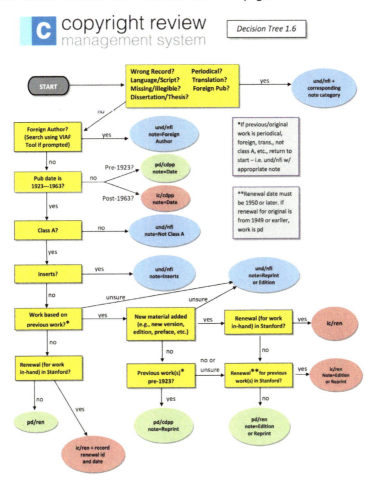

Figure 21 CRMS-US decision tree

APPENDICES

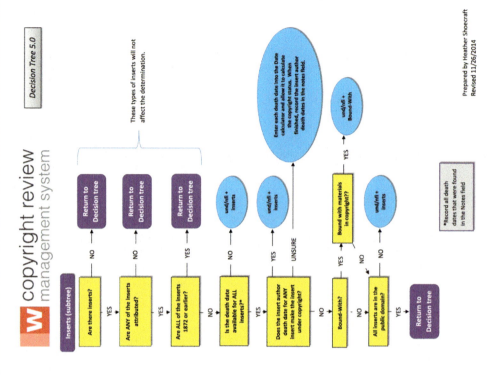

Figures 22 & 23 CRMS-World decision tree

APPENDICES

Name of Institution:		PG	
Contact:		Principal Investigator	
Address:		Total Cost-Share Commitment	-
City, State, and Zip:			

Project Title: **"CRMS-World"**

Remit to: Project Start Date   12/1/14
University of Michigan Libraries   End Date   2/28/16

Date	Expenditures for the Period		
1/1/15	12/1/2014 - 12/31/2014		
Expense Category Description		**Current Expense (this month)**	**Cumulative Expense (since 12/1/2014)**
Faculty Salaries (direct costs)			
Reviewer's name (PERCENTAGE OF TIME IN REVIEWERS' SCHEDULE)			
Staff Salaries (direct costs)			
Reviewer's name (PERCENTAGE OF TIME IN REVIEWERS' SCHEDULE)			
Fringe Benefits			
Reviewer's name (PERCENTAGE OF TIME IN REVIEWERS' SCHEDULE)			
(Please do NOT include Indirect Costs in this report.)			
	Current Total	-	
	Cumulative Total		-

"I certify that to the best of my knowledge all expeditures reported are for appropriate purposes and in accordance with the agreements set forth in the application and award documents"

Authorized Administrative Signature

Figure 24 Cost-share report template

APPENDICES

Job Description
CRMS-World Reviewer

For individual personnel files as desired		
Reviewer Name:		
Institution:		
FTE % assignment		Date
Hours per week		

Thank you for participating in this exciting opportunity to help identify public domain works. This document lays out the expectations and job description for reviewers working on the Copyright Review Management System (CRMS) which is an IMLS grant funded activity to investigate the copyright status of digitized works in HathiTrust, a shared digital repository for research libraries.[1] Reviewers are designated by their institution to participate at a percentage of time based on the cost-share commitment each institution has made to IMLS.

A CRMS reviewer performs the following:

- Verifies accuracy of bibliographic information for works under copyright status review;
- Sends feedback to HathiTrust as necessary (i.e. the scan fails to match the bibliographic item);
- Using jurisdiction-specific online databases, identifies the death date of the author(s) of a given work. Makes appropriate note of the resources used to identify relevant author information;
- Searches the work for "inserts" (content by another author or contributor that may still be under copyright protection).

Each review is one of at least two that will be performed for each work. Wherever legally possible, the books identified as public domain will be made accessible in HathiTrust. It is the responsibility of a CRMS reviewer to be diligent in their assessment and to follow the procedural guidelines set out in the CRMS decision tree and wiki. It is essential that the reviewer pay close attention to detail and ask for feedback whenever a question arises regarding CRMS processes. A reviewer is responsible for following basic security protocol when being given special access to potentially in-copyright book scans, including not sharing their password or using access for a purpose other than copyright review.[2] A reviewer can work more or less in any given week, but the overall effort must accomplish the total by the end of this grant period (2/28/2016).

Skills required: Ability to read and follow directions; fine attention to detail; database research skills; geographic knowledge sufficient to identify works published outside of the UK, Canada, and Australia; ability to make independent judgments based on information collected during the review process; conceptual understanding of bibliographic records and frontmatter of a book is preferred.

---
[1] Grant website: http://www.lib.umich.edu/imls-national-leadership-grant-crms-world
[2] Security expectations are laid out in the Statement for Access Form signed by all reviewers

Version 1/2015

Figure 25 Job description of CRMS-World reviewer

APPENDICES

Job Description
CRMS Expert Reviewer

Expert Name:	
Institution:	
FTE % assign.	Date
Hours per week	

Copyright Review Management System (CRMS) expert reviewers perform an essential project administration and auditing function for the CRMS system. The CRMS Project Team selects expert reviewers from the pool of copyright reviewers at CRMS partner institutions. Expert reviewers demonstrate a consistent level of volume and quality of reviews in CRMS, along with particularly careful attention to detail and demonstrated reasonable, consistent, and reliable judgment. CRMS expert reviewers are careful and conservative in their approach to reviews, making them ideally suited to adjudicating conflicting reviews.

In addition to adjudicating reviewer conflicts and prudently resolving them in line with CRMS guidance, the expert reviewer contributes valuable additional rights research, enhances the integrity and reliability of CRMS, and promotes the smooth operation of the system.

The CRMS expert reviewer:

- Uses conservative judgment and knowledge of CRMS guidelines to resolve conflicting reviews from CRMS reviewers, by examining the digital scan of the reviewed work and checking reviewer determinations, including all relevant review notes. Performs additional research as needed.
- Selects correct reviews, makes corrections to reviews when applicable, and adds research notes whenever relevant.
- Invalidates reviews as necessary.
- May submit an entirely new review, based on the expert reviewer's unique review and research into the copyright status of the work.
- Performs independent research, including verification of author death dates for the reviewed work.
- Determines the reliability of death date resources identified by CRMS reviewers.
- Works closely with the University of Michigan CRMS team and reports any observed pattern of inaccurate reviews from CRMS reviewers.
- Provides valuable feedback to CRMS in order to improve the system and address ambiguities in CRMS processes and guidance.
- Shares insights with CRMS reviewers through teaching, revisions to the CRMS Wiki, and other communications to the group.

Updated 12/2014

Wherever legally possible, the books that expert reviewers identify as public domain will be made accessible in HathiTrust. Expert reviewers are diligent in their assessment and follow the procedural guidelines set out in the CRMS Decision Tree and CRMS Wiki. Expert reviewers pay close attention to detail and ask for feedback whenever CRMS processes are unclear. Finally, expert reviewers follow CRMS security protocols when being given special access to potentially in-copyright book scans, including not sharing their passwords or using access for a purpose other than copyright review.

Skills required: Database research skills; deep understanding of CRMS processes; strong analytical skills and excellent judgment (critical); geographic knowledge sufficient to identify works published outside of the UK, Canada, and Australia; fine attention to detail; ability to make independent judgments based on information collected during the review process.

Updated 12/2014

Figures 26 & 27 Job description of CRMS expert reviewer

APPENDICES

RIGHTS AND REASON CODES

CRMS rights/reason codes are a key part of our documentation. They refer to the copyright determination we have made for the work, and HathiTrust translates them into access decisions.

CRMS-US and CRMS-World rights/reason codes are as follows:

CRMS-US

Rights/reason	Description
pd/ren	Public domain based on no renewal
pd/cdpp	Public domain based on pre-1923 publication
pd/ncn	Public domain based on no copyright notice
ic/ren	In copyright; copyright renewed
ic/cdpp	In copyright, or undetermined, based on post-1963 publication
und/nfi	Undetermined; needs further investigation

APPENDICES

CRMS-WORLD

Rights/reason	Description
pd/add	Public domain based on author's death date
pd/exp	Public domain based on publication date
pdus/add	Public domain in the United States; not public domain outside of the United States based on author's death date
ic/add	In copyright based on author's death date
icus/gatt	In copyright in the United States due to GATT restoration; in the public domain in country of origin based on author's death date
und/nfi	Undetermined; needs further investigation

Access

The following forms of access are provided via HathiTrust, based on the copyright determination made for the volume.

PD US

Public domain US determinations apply only to access in the United States. A typical example of a PD US determination would be a pre-1923 publication that may be subject to copyright in other countries. US-based users, as determined by IP address, would be able to access these works, but they would not be more broadly accessible.

APPENDICES

PD Worldwide

PD Worldwide determinations apply throughout the world, no matter where the user is coming from. A simple example of a PD Worldwide decision is a work published prior to 1875, where CRMS and HathiTrust have decided that the work has entered the public domain regardless of legal regime.

IC US/PD Worldwide

This designation is primarily used when we can provide access to the work outside of the United States but, due to copyright restoration, we cannot provide access to the work within the United States. Here, imagine a work first published in the United Kingdom in 1930, then published (and not renewed) in the United States in 1932. The author died in 1940. This work would be in the public domain in the United Kingdom based on the author death date, but its copyright would be restored in the United States. In the United States, the work would not enter the public domain until January 1, 2028 (1932 + 95 years).

UND/NFI

The und/nfi category has no impact on the bibliographic record–based access to the work. It is a determination that draws attention to the need for additional research.

EXCERPTS FROM THE CRMS-WORLD WIKI

A password-protected wiki was used as a knowledge base to document commonly occurring questions and scenarios. It contained instructions

APPENDICES

specific to the CRMS project scope, workflow procedures, and interface. During the first two grant years, reviewers encountered new questions more frequently. Following that time period, the wiki content did not require as many updates and remained stable other than for a content reorganization to improve cross references and searchability.

Structurally the pages were divided into either reference answers dealing with decision-making processes or technical help with the interface. The main page menu is shown here along with a sample set of entries to give an idea of the design. Individual entries are specific to CRMS workflow. This sample is provided as a model for organizing and documenting information because the knowledge base for any given project must be designed to meet the specific needs and scope of that project.

Figure 28 Front page of the CRMS wiki

APPENDICES

Single Authorship

Works with a single author or a single editor are presumably the easiest to review. Enter the author's death date into the date field, and try to confirm the death date in two sources. Make a note of the sources in the note field.

>Date field: *Author death date*
>Rights/reason code: *Let the system calculate*
>Note category: *Date*
>Notes field example: *Author death date in Virtual International Authority File (VIAF), Zephir*

Author Death Date Not Found

If you are unable to locate the author's death date, mark the work und/nfi. There is no need to document all the sources you checked.

>Date field: *Leave blank*
>Rights/reason code: und/nfi
>Note category: *Date*
>Notes field example: *No death date found*

Do not use the publication date when you are unable to find an author death date, as this will cause errors in the rights/reason code.

APPENDICES

Approximate Death Dates

If an author has dates listed as fl./flourished or c./circa, the dates should be considered approximate. If the approximate date is 1840 or earlier, you may use the approximate date in place of an author death date. If the approximate date is 1841 or later, do not calculate the copyright status using the approximate date. Unless you are able to locate the exact death date, mark the work und/nfi.

Author Name Missing from Title Page

If there is an author listed in the catalog record but not on the title page or other front matter, trust the information in the catalog record and review as normal.

Late Author

If the title page indicates the author is deceased and it seems clear the author died prior to publication, you may use the publication date in place of the author death date if the actual death date cannot be found. Make a note of your reasoning in the note field.

Foreign Language Works with English Front Matter

This can be a nuanced decision process and outcomes may vary. Please document your analysis in the notes field so that an expert can evaluate it.

APPENDICES

The presence of a foreign language alone does not preclude a copyright determination, but we are most concerned with the possibility of reviewers missing copyright-relevant information in non-English-language front matter. If the front matter of the volume is in English, the body is in a foreign language, and you feel confident assessing the copyright status of the entire work, you may proceed. If in doubt, mark it und/nfi as a foreign language work.

Compilations and Anthologies

Sometimes the bibliographic record lists a personal author when the work is actually a compilation from many various authors. Examples would be conference proceedings with articles by multiple authors, compiled poetry from many poets, or anthologies.

> Date field: *Use author death date (rely on the catalog record to tell who is the main author)*
> Rights/reason code: *und/nfi*
> Note category: *Insert(s)*
> Notes field example: *Multiple contributors*

If there are five or more contributors, leave it and move on rather than searching for all their death dates.

APPENDICES

Sheet Music or Musical Compositions

Although musical works get the same copyright treatment of life + 70 years in the UK, we are making it a policy to set aside any musical works. The reason for this is caution for additional authorship from lyricists and arrangers.

Date field: *Composer's death date*
Rights/reason code: *und/nfi*
Note category: *Music*
Notes field example: *Musical score*

CRMS-WORLD TRAINING TEST 1

The two test modules displayed here were used as part of the CRMS training program to evaluate new reviewer learning and comprehension. We used the Qualtrics platform, which is primarily software for creating surveys. With the addition of answer validation capabilities, it became a lightweight method for testing. Trainees were able to consult the CRMS wiki and other reference materials in order to answer the questions. They needed to demonstrate proficiency through these tests before being authorized to do practice reviews within the CRMS sandbox interface.

APPENDICES

PART 1—PROJECT SCOPE

Q1
What countries are "in scope" for the CRMS-World project?
- ○ UK only
- ○ UK and Canada
- ○ UK, Canada, Ireland, and Australia

Q2
Unpublished works are
- ○ In scope
- ○ Out of scope because our legal assumptions only apply to published works

Q3
Which of the following are *true* statements about how we choose the scope of publication dates to work on?
- ○ Our range includes books up until about 1946 (current year minus seventy) and not later for UK works because the likelihood of finding public domain books drops off sharply since authors are not likely to have died before publishing.
- ○ Our scope of dates rolls forward by one year every January 1st.
- ○ Books published 1874 or earlier are automatically marked as public domain worldwide by the HathiTrust via a bibliographic determination. We do not need to review them. (This date rolls forward by one every year.)
- ○ The latest date we currently review is up to 1966 for Canada and Australia (current year minus fifty).

APPENDICES

Q4
Decision Tree / Workflow

For a book having a single personal author (and no inserts), what is the order of steps you would take in making a review? Number the following from 1 to 7:

_____ Search for an author death date and enter it into the date field

_____ Verify that the catalog record matches the scan you see

_____ Verify author death date in a second source (if possible)

_____ Submit the determination

_____ Verify that the publisher is British, Australian, or Canadian

_____ Rule out dissertations, translations, dictionaries, encyclopedias, and US publications

_____ Select a note category and type death date sources and any additional info into the Notes field

Q5
Personal Authors

For a book having a personal author, what date is used to determine the length of copyright term?

○ Death of the last living author

○ Publication date

Q6
Corporate Authors with a Named Individual Author

For a book appearing to have corporate authorship and a named individual author, how is the length of the copyright term calculated?

○ Seventy years after the death of the author

○ Seventy years from the publication date if UK; fifty years from publication date if Australia or Canada

APPENDICES

Q7

Corporate Authors without a Named Individual Author

For a book appearing to have corporate authorship and no named individual author, how is the length of the copyright term calculated?

- ○ Seventy years after the death of the author
- ○ Seventy years from the publication date if UK; fifty years from publication date if Australia or Canada

Q8

Crown Copyright

For a book having Crown copyright, how is the length of the copyright term calculated?

- ○ Seventy years after the death of the author
- ○ Fifty years from the publication date

PART 2—UNDETERMINED WORKS

This is a series of questions asking what should be marked as undetermined (und/nfi) or what is OK to proceed with as a review. Please use the CRMS wiki to look up answers.

Q9

Works that are out of scope should be set aside rather than making a final copyright determination. For which of these situations would you choose a und/nfi code?

	und/nfi	OK to proceed
Published in the United States	○	○
Published in Ireland	○	○
Published in Australia	○	○
Published in Canada	○	○
Published in the UK	○	○

APPENDICES

Q10

Works that lack crucial information should be set aside rather than making a final copyright determination. For which of these situations would you choose a und/nfi code?

	und/nfi	OK to proceed
Title page appears to be completely missing from the scan	○	○
Publication date is missing from the title page, but there is a publication date given in the catalog record	○	○
There's an image caption, but the image itself appears to be missing	○	○

Q11

Certain types of publications are complicated and should be set aside rather than making a final copyright determination. For which of these situations would you choose a und/nfi code?

	und/nfi	OK to proceed
Work is a dissertation, encyclopedia, or dictionary	○	○
Work is a scientific report	○	○
Work is a play or poetry	○	○
Work is an auction catalog	○	○
Work is a collection of speeches given by one author	○	○

APPENDICES

Q12

Certain types of publications are complicated and should be set aside rather than making a final copyright determination. For which of these situations would you choose a und/nfi code?

	und/nfi	OK to proceed
There are upward of five authors/contributors	○	○
Language contains classical text (e.g., Greek passages) that are in the original language	○	○
Language is a translation from French, Italian, German, etc.	○	○
Work contains segments by the author reprinted from earlier publications such as journals	○	○
Author is not corporate and no author name is given (i.e., anonymous)	○	○
Author is actually an editor, and the volume is "collected works" by various authors	○	○

PART 3—INSERTS

This section is related to inserts. You'll go through a series of questions asking what should be marked und/nfi or what is OK to proceed. Please use the CRMS wiki to look up answers as you go.

APPENDICES

Q13

Depending on the death date information that you find (or don't find), coauthors or illustrators might cause a book to be set aside into und/nfi rather than proceeding with a final copyright determination. For which of these situations would you choose a und/nfi code?

	und/nfi	OK to proceed
Three coauthors: you found all three death dates	○	○
Three coauthors: you found two death dates but not the third	○	○
Illustrator's death date is not found	○	○
Author died in 1960s (in copyright) and illustrator died in 1970s (in copyright)	○	○

APPENDICES

Q14

Works that contain potentially copyrightable material by someone other than the author are deemed to have inserts. In some cases, inserts need not affect the outcome; in some cases (perhaps 30 percent of reviews), they require us to set aside a work for further investigation rather than making a final copyright determination. For which of these insert situations would you choose a und/nfi code?

	und/nfi	OK to proceed
Photograph credited to a photo studio (as a corporate work); publication date is prior to 1925	○	○
Collection of letters and correspondence dated pre-1872—various authors	○	○
Foreword written in a Crown copyright work	○	○
Museum collection paintings from the 1700s	○	○
Preface written by an editor (no death date found)	○	○
Credited list of illustrations (many people contributing)	○	○
Introductory chapter written by another author (his death date is found and puts the work in copyright)	○	○

APPENDICES

PART 4—AUTHOR DEATH DATES

This section contains a few short questions related to searching for a death date.

Q15

We import some death dates for your convenience, but it's important to know how they work. For about 50 percent of your reviews, you will notice a death date that has been imported from the Zephir record or from VIAF. The Zephir import is trustworthy, as it connects directly with the catalog record. You still should look up a secondary source as well to verify. When a death date has been imported from VIAF, however, that is merely based on a fuzzy name search of VIAF. In many cases, it has connected to the wrong person. Whenever you see the red-letter indication that a date is importing from VIAF, you should be sure to check VIAF and to confirm that it is referring to the right person.

○ OK, I understand.
○ I'm not sure what you're talking about. Let's go over this.

Q16

The data sources for the author's death date (i.e., Zephir, VIAF, Wikipedia, COPAC, website URL)

○ Should be entered into the notes field
○ Don't need to be noted

Q17

If a death date has been automatically imported from VIAF, do you need to go to VIAF and verify that it matches the right person?

○ Yes
○ No

APPENDICES

Q18

Which resource is useful for disambiguating a common name by also searching on the book title?
- ○ LoC Authorities
- ○ NGCOBA
- ○ COPAC

Q19

What resource is primarily for Canadian authors?
- ○ AMICUS
- ○ AustLit
- ○ LoC Authorities

Q20

What can help determine that you have the correct death date for this "John Smith" and not the wrong "John Smith"? Select all that could help:
- ○ The VIAF record shows a history of publishing on the same subject matter as the particular book in hand.
- ○ He was born prior to the publication date on the book.
- ○ Wikipedia lists that particular book title on his entry.
- ○ A cataloger has added his death date to the bibliographic record / WorldCat Identities record associated with that particular book.

APPENDICES

CRMS-WORLD TRAINING TEST 2

PART I—BASIC REVIEWS

The following examples are intended to be straightforward and answerable using the information that has been provided.

Example 1: Use the images below to answer the following questions. Assume there is no other relevant information in the front matter of this work.

Title page

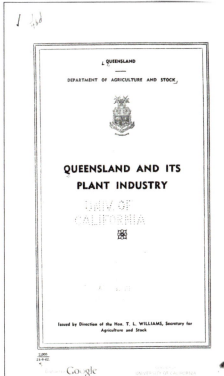

Bibliographic record

ID: uc1.$b69122
Title: Queensland and its plant industry
Author: Queensland. Dept. of Agriculture and Stok
Pub Date: 1942
Country: Australia

APPENDICES

Determine the authorship of this work.
- ◯ Single author
- ◯ Corporate author
- ◯ Anonymous
- ◯ Crown copyright

How would you make the determination? Select the appropriate choice.
- ◯ Enter the author's death date and let the system calculate
- ◯ Pull the publication date and let the system calculate
- ◯ Manually select und/nfi

Enter the appropriate date. If a date is not required, please leave this question blank.

Select the appropriate note category. Not all reviews will require a note category. If a note category is not required, please select "none" from the list below.
- ◯ None
- ◯ Author
- ◯ Crown copyright
- ◯ Date
- ◯ Dissertation/thesis
- ◯ Edition
- ◯ Expert note
- ◯ Insert(s)
- ◯ Language
- ◯ Misc.
- ◯ Missing
- ◯ Reprint
- ◯ Translation
- ◯ Wrong record

APPENDICES

For the Notes field, what notes would you enter? Not all reviews will require you to add a note. If that is the case, please leave this question blank.

Example 2: Use the title page and the bibliographic record to answer the following questions. Assume there is no other relevant information in the front matter of this work.

Title page

> THE ART OF MARBLING
> AND
> Treatment of the New Bronze Colours.
>
> A PRACTICAL GUIDE
> TO
> MARBLING BY HALFER'S METHOD
>
> WITH 26 SPECIMENS OF MARBLING, SOME OF WHICH ARE GELATINISED, ALSO ILLUSTRATIONS
>
> SECOND IMPROVED AND ENLARGED EDITION
> PRICE 5/-
>
> LONDON 1904.
> Published by THE HOSTMANN PRINTING INK CO., LTD.
> 13/14, Great Sutton Street, London, E.C.
> ENTERED AT STATIONER'S HALL.

Bibliographic record

ID: mdp.39015078080622
Title: The art of marbling & treatment of new bronze colours
Author:
Pub Date: 1904
Country: United Kingdom

APPENDICES

Determine the authorship of this work.
- ○ Single author
- ○ Corporate author
- ○ Anonymous
- ○ Crown copyright

How would you make the determination? Select the appropriate choice.
- ○ Enter the author's death date and let the system calculate
- ○ Pull the publication date and let the system calculate
- ○ Manually select und/nfi

Enter the appropriate date. If a date is not required, please leave this question blank.

Select the appropriate note category. Not all reviews will require a note category. If a note category is not required, please select "none" from the list below.
- ○ None
- ○ Author
- ○ Crown copyright
- ○ Date
- ○ Dissertation/thesis
- ○ Edition
- ○ Expert note
- ○ Insert(s)
- ○ Language
- ○ Misc.
- ○ Missing
- ○ Reprint
- ○ Translation
- ○ Wrong record

APPENDICES

For the Notes field, what notes would you enter? Not all reviews will require you to add a note. If that is the case, please leave this question blank.

Example 3: Use the images below to answer the following questions. Assume there is no other relevant information in the front matter of this work.

Title page

Bibliographic record

ID: bc.ark/13960/t0000n50w
Title: Ireland in 1921
Author: Street, Cecil J. C.
Pub Date: 1922
Country: United Kingdom

VIAF record

APPENDICES

Determine the authorship of this work.
- ○ Single author
- ○ Corporate author
- ○ Anonymous
- ○ Crown copyright

How would you make the determination? Select the appropriate choice.
- ○ Enter the author's death date and let the system calculate
- ○ Pull the publication date and let the system calculate
- ○ Manually select und/nfi

Enter the appropriate date. If a date is not required, please leave this question blank.

Select the appropriate note category. Not all reviews will require a note category. If a note category is not required, please select "none" from the list below.
- ○ None
- ○ Author
- ○ Crown copyright
- ○ Date
- ○ Dissertation/thesis
- ○ Edition
- ○ Expert note
- ○ Insert(s)
- ○ Language
- ○ Misc.
- ○ Missing
- ○ Reprint
- ○ Translation
- ○ Wrong record

APPENDICES

For the Notes field, what notes would you enter? Not all reviews will require you to add a note. If that is the case, please leave this question blank.

Example 4: Use the images below to answer the following questions. Assume there is no other relevant information in the front matter of this work.

Title page

Bibliographic record

ID: coo.31924000252100
Title: The meningococcus
Author: Murray, Everitt George Dunne
Pub Date: 1929
Country: United Kingdom

VIAF record for Murray

Murray, E. G. D.
Murray, E. G. D. (Everitt George Dunne), 1890–1964
Murray, Everitt D. G.
Murray, Everitt George Dunne, nar. 1890
Murray, Everitt George Dunne, 1890–1964
VIAF ID: 84822170 (Personal)
Permalink: http://viaf.org/viaf/84822170
ISNI-test: 0000 0001 2018 4466

APPENDICES

Determine the authorship of this work.
- ◯ Single author
- ◯ Corporate author
- ◯ Anonymous
- ◯ Crown copyright

How would you make the determination? Select the appropriate choice.
- ◯ Enter the author's death date and let the system calculate
- ◯ Pull the publication date and let the system calculate
- ◯ Manually select und/nfi

Enter the appropriate date. If a date is not required, please leave this question blank.

Select the appropriate note category. Not all reviews will require a note category. If a note category is not required, please select "none" from the list below.
- ◯ None
- ◯ Author
- ◯ Crown copyright
- ◯ Date
- ◯ Dissertation/thesis
- ◯ Edition
- ◯ Expert note
- ◯ Insert(s)
- ◯ Language
- ◯ Misc.
- ◯ Missing
- ◯ Reprint
- ◯ Translation
- ◯ Wrong record

APPENDICES

For the Notes field, what notes would you enter? Not all reviews will require you to add a note. If that is the case, please leave this question blank.

PART II—BEYOND THE BASICS

Example 5: Use the image below to answer the following questions. Assume there is no other relevant information to be found. These are the first eight pages of the book (no other front matter exists).

There are no other pages in the front matter of this work. Is anything missing?

How would you make the determination? Select the appropriate choice.
- ○ Enter the author's death date and let the system calculate
- ○ Pull the publication date and let the system calculate
- ○ Manually select und/nfi

APPENDICES

Select the appropriate note category. Not all reviews will require a note category. If a note category is not required, please select "none" from the list below.

- ○ None
- ○ Author
- ○ Crown copyright
- ○ Date
- ○ Dissertation/thesis
- ○ Edition
- ○ Expert note
- ○ Insert(s)
- ○ Language
- ○ Misc.
- ○ Missing
- ○ Reprint
- ○ Translation
- ○ Wrong record

For the Notes field, what notes would you enter? Not all reviews will require you to add a note. If that is the case, please leave this question blank.

Should feedback be reported?
- ○ Report feedback
- ○ No feedback required

What feedback would you enter? If feedback is not required, please leave this question blank.

APPENDICES

Example 6: Use the image below to answer the following questions. Assume there is no other relevant information to be found.

Title page

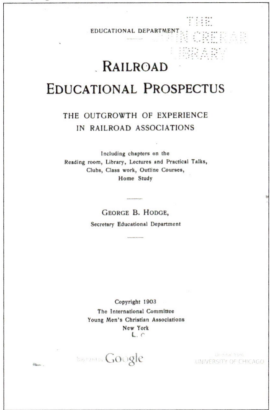

Determine the authorship of this work.
- ○ Single author
- ○ Corporate author
- ○ Anonymous
- ○ Crown copyright

APPENDICES

How would you make the determination? Select the appropriate choice.
- ○ Enter the author's death date and let the system calculate
- ○ Pull the publication date and let the system calculate
- ○ Manually select und/nfi

Select the appropriate note category. Not all reviews will require a note category. If a note category is not required, please select "none" from the list below.
- ○ None
- ○ Author
- ○ Crown copyright
- ○ Date
- ○ Dissertation/thesis
- ○ Edition
- ○ Expert note
- ○ Insert(s)
- ○ Language
- ○ Misc.
- ○ Missing
- ○ Reprint
- ○ Translation
- ○ Wrong record

For the Notes field, what notes would you enter? Not all reviews will require you to add a note. If that is the case, leave this question blank.

Should feedback be reported?
- ○ Report feedback
- ○ No feedback required

What feedback would you enter? If feedback is not required, please leave this question blank.

APPENDICES

Example 7: Use the image below to answer the following questions. Assume there is no other relevant information to be found.

Title page

>
> CHAPTERS IN THE HISTORY
> OF SCIENCE
> General Editor CHARLES SINGER
>
> II
>
> *Mathematics and Physical Science in Classical Antiquity*
>
> Translated from the German
> of
> J. L. Heiberg
> by
> D. C. Macgregor
>
> LONDON
> OXFORD UNIVERSITY PRESS
> Humphrey Milford
> 1922

Determine the authorship of this work.
- ◯ Single author
- ◯ Corporate author
- ◯ Anonymous
- ◯ Crown copyright

How would you make the determination? Select the appropriate choice.
- ◯ Enter the author's death date and let the system calculate
- ◯ Pull the publication date and let the system calculate
- ◯ Manually select und/nfi

APPENDICES

Select the appropriate note category. Not all reviews will require a note category. If a note category is not required, please select "none" from the list below.

- ○ None
- ○ Author
- ○ Crown copyright
- ○ Date
- ○ Dissertation/thesis
- ○ Edition
- ○ Expert note
- ○ Insert(s)
- ○ Language
- ○ Misc.
- ○ Missing
- ○ Reprint
- ○ Translation
- ○ Wrong record

For the Notes field, what notes would you enter? Not all reviews will require you to add a note. If that is the case, leave this question blank.

Should feedback be reported?
- ○ Report feedback
- ○ No feedback required

What feedback would you enter? If feedback is not required, leave this question blank.

APPENDICES

Example 8: Use the images below to answer the following questions. Assume there is no other relevant information to be found.

Title page

The Cambridge Bible for Schools
GENERAL EDITOR:—J. J. S. PEROWNE, D.D.,
DEAN OF PETERBOROUGH.

THE GENERAL EPISTLES OF

ST PETER & ST JUDE,

WITH NOTES AND INTRODUCTION

BY

E. H. PLUMPTRE, D.D.,

PROFESSOR OF NEW TESTAMENT EXEGESIS, KING'S COLLEGE, LONDON; VICAR OF BICKLEY.

EDITED FOR THE SYNDICS OF THE UNIVERSITY PRESS.

Cambridge:
AT THE UNIVERSITY PRESS.
London: CAMBRIDGE WAREHOUSE, 17, PATERNOSTER ROW
Cambridge: DEIGHTON, BELL, AND CO.
1879
[All Rights reserved.]

Table of contents

CONTENTS.

		PAGES
I.	INTRODUCTION.	
	Chapter I. The training of the Disciple	5—33
	Chapter II. The work of the Apostle	33—53
	Chapter III. The traditions of the Church	53—59
	Chapter IV. The First Epistle:	
	(1) The readers of the Epistle	60—62
	(2) The time and place of the Epistle	62—64
	(3) Analysis of Contents	64—72
	Chapter V. The Second Epistle :	
	(1) Question of authorship	73—78
	(2) Occasion and date	79—81
	(3) Analysis of Contents	81—83
	Chapter VI. The Life of St Jude	83—88
	Chapter VII. The Epistle of St Jude	88—90
II.	TEXT AND NOTES	91—217
III.	INDEX	218

. The Text adopted in this Edition is that of Dr Scrivener's *Cambridge Paragraph Bible*. A few variations from the ordinary Text, chiefly in the spelling of certain words, and in the use of italics, will be noticed. For the principles adopted by Dr Scrivener as regards the printing of the Text see his Introduction to the *Paragraph Bible*, published by the Cambridge University Press.

Determine the authorship of this work.
- ◯ Single author
- ◯ Corporate author
- ◯ Anonymous
- ◯ Crown copyright

How would you make the determination? Select the appropriate choice.
- ◯ Enter the author's death date and let the system calculate
- ◯ Pull the publication date and let the system calculate
- ◯ Manually select und/nfi

APPENDICES

Select the appropriate note category. Not all reviews will require a note category. If a note category is not required, please select "none" from the list below.

- ○ None
- ○ Author
- ○ Crown copyright
- ○ Date
- ○ Dissertation/thesis
- ○ Edition
- ○ Expert note
- ○ Insert(s)
- ○ Language
- ○ Misc.
- ○ Missing
- ○ Reprint
- ○ Translation
- ○ Wrong record

For the Notes field, what notes would you enter? Not all reviews will require you to add a note. If that is the case, leave this question blank.

Should feedback be reported?
- ○ Report feedback
- ○ No feedback required

What feedback would you enter? If feedback is not required, leave this question blank.

APPENDICES

Example 9: Use the image below to answer the following questions. Assume there is no other relevant information to be found.

Title page

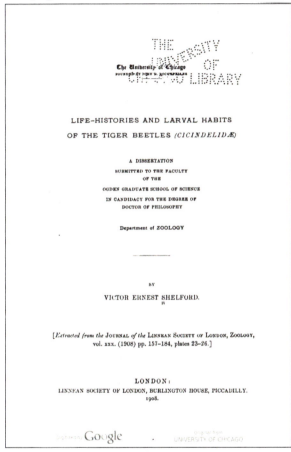

Determine the authorship of this work.
- ○ Single author
- ○ Corporate author
- ○ Anonymous
- ○ Crown copyright

APPENDICES

How would you make the determination? Select the appropriate choice.
- ○ Enter the author's death date and let the system calculate
- ○ Pull the publication date and let the system calculate
- ○ Manually select und/nfi

Select the appropriate note category. Not all reviews will require a note category. If one is not required, select "none" from the list below.
- ○ None
- ○ Author
- ○ Crown copyright
- ○ Date
- ○ Dissertation/thesis
- ○ Edition
- ○ Expert note
- ○ Insert(s)
- ○ Language
- ○ Misc.
- ○ Missing
- ○ Reprint
- ○ Translation
- ○ Wrong record

For the Notes field, what notes would you enter? Not all reviews will require you to add a note. If that is the case, leave this question blank.

Should feedback be reported?
- ○ Report feedback
- ○ No feedback required

What feedback would you enter? If feedback is not required, leave this question blank.

APPENDICES

Example 10: Use the image below to answer the following questions. Assume there is no other relevant information to be found.

Title page

> A
>
> SMALLER DICTIONARY
>
> OF
>
> Greek and Roman Antiquities.
>
> BY WILLIAM SMITH, D.C.L., LL.D.,
> EDITOR OF THE 'CLASSICAL AND LATIN DICTIONARIES,' ETC.
>
> ABRIDGED FROM THE LARGER DICTIONARY.
>
> THIRTEENTH EDITION.
>
> ILLUSTRATED WITH TWO HUNDRED WOODCUTS.
>
> LONDON:

Determine the authorship of this work.
- ○ Single author
- ○ Corporate author
- ○ Anonymous
- ○ Crown copyright

APPENDICES

How would you make the determination? Select the appropriate choice.
- ○ Enter the author's death date and let the system calculate
- ○ Pull the publication date and let the system calculate
- ○ Manually select und/nfi

Select the appropriate note category. Not all reviews will require a note category. If a note category is not required, please select "none" from the list below.
- ○ None
- ○ Author
- ○ Crown copyright
- ○ Date
- ○ Dissertation/thesis
- ○ Edition
- ○ Expert note
- ○ Insert(s)
- ○ Language
- ○ Misc.
- ○ Missing
- ○ Reprint
- ○ Translation
- ○ Wrong record

For the Notes field, what notes would you enter? Not all reviews will require you to add a note. If that is the case, leave this question blank.

Should feedback be reported?
- ○ Report feedback
- ○ No feedback required

What feedback would you enter? If feedback is not required, leave this question blank.

APPENDICES

Example 11: Use the image below to answer the following questions. Assume there is no other relevant information to be found.

Title page

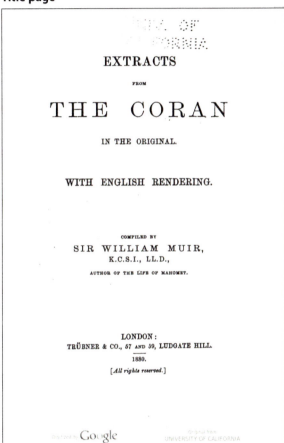

Determine the authorship of this work.
- ○ Single author
- ○ Corporate author
- ○ Anonymous
- ○ Crown copyright

APPENDICES

How would you make the determination? Select the appropriate choice.
- ◯ Enter the author's death date and let the system calculate
- ◯ Pull the publication date and let the system calculate
- ◯ Manually select und/nfi

Select the appropriate note category. Not all reviews will require a note category. If a note category is not required, please select "none" from the list below.
- ◯ None
- ◯ Author
- ◯ Crown copyright
- ◯ Date
- ◯ Dissertation/thesis
- ◯ Edition
- ◯ Expert note
- ◯ Insert(s)
- ◯ Language
- ◯ Misc.
- ◯ Missing
- ◯ Reprint
- ◯ Translation
- ◯ Wrong record

For the Notes field, what notes would you enter? Not all reviews will require you to add a note. If that is the case, leave this question blank.

Should feedback be reported?
- ◯ Report feedback
- ◯ No feedback required

What feedback would you enter? If feedback is not required, leave this question blank.

APPENDICES

PART III—MULTIPLE AUTHORS AND INSERTS

Example 12: Use the images below to answer the following questions. Assume there is no other relevant information to be found.

Title page

> EDINBURGH CASTLE
>
> THE BUILDINGS
> By J. S. RICHARDSON, F.S.A. Scot.
> Inspector of Ancient Monuments for Scotland
>
> HISTORY
> By MARGUERITE WOOD, M.A., Ph.D.
> Keeper of the Burgh Records
>
> EDINBURGH
> HIS MAJESTY'S STATIONERY OFFICE
> 1933
>
> 70-272

Bibliographic record

ID: mdp.39015027321382
Title: Edinburgh castle
Author: Richardson, J. S.
Pub Date: 1933
Country: United Kingdom

VIAF records indicate that Richardson, J. S., died in 1970 and Wood, Marguerite, died in 1954. Which death date would you record in the author death date field?

○ 1954 (Wood, Marguerite)
○ 1970 (Richardson, J. S.)
○ Either date

Explain your choice.

APPENDICES

Example 13: Use the images below to answer the following questions. Assume there is no other relevant information to be found.

Title page

SOILS IN CANADA

Geological, Pedological, and Engineering Studies

THE ROYAL SOCIETY OF CANADA, SPECIAL PUBLICATIONS, NO. 3

Edited by Robert F. Legget

PUBLISHED BY THE UNIVERSITY OF TORONTO PRESS IN CO-OPERATION WITH THE ROYAL SOCIETY OF CANADA
1961

Table of contents

CONTENTS

Preface		v
Introduction	R. F. LEGGET, F.R.S.C.	3
Geology of the Soils of Canada	V. K. PREST, F.R.S.C.	6
Soils of the Coastal Area of Southwest British Columbia	J. E. ARMSTRONG, F.R.S.C.	22
Glacial Deposits of Alberta	C. P. GRAVENOR and L. A. BAYROCK	33
Soils of the Lake Agassiz Region	JOHN A. ELSON	51
Tills of Southern Ontario	ALEKSIS DREIMANIS	80
The Champlain Sea and Its Sediments	P. F. KARROW	97
Glacial Geology and the Soils of Nova Scotia	H. L. CAMERON	109
Organic Terrain	NORMAN W. RADFORTH, F.R.S.C.	115
Clay Mineralogy of Canadian Soils	S. A. FORMAN and J. E. BRYDON	140
The Soils of Canada from a Pedological Viewpoint	A. LEAHEY	147
Characteristics and Genesis of Podzol Soils	P. C. STOBBE	158
Genesis and Characteristics of Solonetzic Soils, With particular reference to those of Alberta, Canada	W. EARL BOWSER	165
The Soils of Southern Ontario	N. R. RICHARDS	174
Correlation of Engineering and Pedological Soil Classification in Ontario	A RUTKA	183
Influence of Geology on the Design and Construction of Airports	NORMAN W. MCLEOD	195

vii

Bibliographic record

ID: mdp.39015010046939
Title: Soils in Canada
Author: Legget, Robert Ferguson
Pub Date: 1961

274

APPENDICES

Determine the authorship of this work.
- ◯ Single author
- ◯ Corporate author
- ◯ Anonymous
- ◯ Crown copyright

How would you make the determination?
- ◯ This is a corporate work published by the Royal Society of Canada. Pull the publication date and let the system calculate.
- ◯ Look up the editor's death date (Legget, Robert Ferguson) and let the system calculate.
- ◯ Manually select und/nfi, as there are too many contributors listed in the table of contents to try to find all the death dates.

Explain your choice.

APPENDICES

Example 14: Use the image below to answer the following question. Assume there is no other relevant information to be found.

Title page

APPENDICES

The main author (Van Wyck, William) died in 1965 per VIAF. The copyright determination for this death date is ic/add. The inserts author (Fish, Horace) died in 1929 per VIAF. The copyright determination for this death date is icus/gatt. After recording both death dates and sources in the notes field, how would you proceed?

○ Record either date in the death date field and let the system calculate. Both determinations are in copyright, so it doesn't matter which date is used.

○ Record Van Wyck's death date in the field and manually select und/nfi. Any time inserts are under copyright, und/nfi must be selected.

APPENDICES

Example 15: Use the images below to answer the following question. Assume there is no other relevant information to be found.

Title page

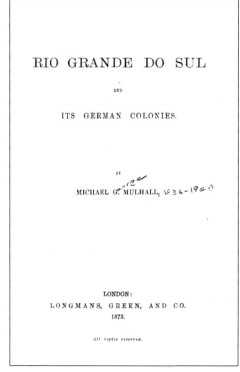

Frontispiece for this work

APPENDICES

Inserts, such as the frontispiece above, can affect the copyright status of a work. Evaluate the image to determine if this illustration would affect the copyright status. For this example, please assume that further information about the frontispiece is not available anywhere else in the scan. Select the best choice below:

- ○ The frontispiece is unattributed. Uncredited inserts are disregarded for the purposes of CRMS.
- ○ The frontispiece is unattributed. Since the insert author's name is unknown, the death date cannot be looked up. (und/nfi should be manually selected.)
- ○ The frontispiece is attributed; finding the insert author's death date would be the next step.

APPENDICES

Example 16: Use the image below to answer the following question. Assume there is no other relevant information to be found.

Title page

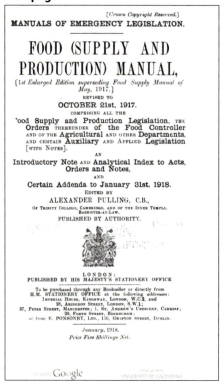

This title page indicates that Crown copyright covers the work, but the title page also lists an editor. Is it necessary to find the death date for the editor (Alexander Pulling)?

○ Yes
○ No

Explain your decision.

APPENDICES

Example 17: Use the image below to answer the following question. Assume there is no other relevant information to be found. This image shows part of a table of contents.

> CONTENTS xi
>
> C. The Preliminary Articles of Peace between Great Britain and France, 20th January 1783 448
> D. The Preliminary Articles of Peace between Great Britain and Spain, 1783 453
>
> APPENDIX II
>
> A. The Visit of the Abbé Morellet to Bowood in 1772, related in his "Memoirs," I, ix 457
> B. Letter of Benjamin Vaughan from Paris to Lord Lansdowne describing the Fête de la Fédération, 15th July 1790 . 462
> C. M. de Talleyrand à Lord Lansdowne . . . 465
> D. Paper on Sepulchral Monuments contributed by Lord Lansdowne to the "Gentleman's Magazine," 1791 . 480
>
> INDEX 483

The table of contents indicates that there are inserts in this work, including a letter and a paper. How would you handle these inserts?

- ○ The inserts predate 1872; therefore they are in the public domain.
- ○ The insert authors' death dates need to be located in VIAF, COPAC, and so on.

- GETTING STARTED
- AT A GLANCE – OVERVIEW
- INVOLVING YOUR LEADERSHIP
- PROJECT SCOPING
- LEGAL
- PERSONNEL
- VERIFICATION
- FUNDING
- TECHNICAL
- PILOT PROJECTS

Glossary

Active volume: A volume in the candidates queue becomes active whenever someone reviews it. Active volumes are given precedence by the queuing algorithm because work has already been done on them. A volume ceases to be active when all parts of the review process are complete.

Admin: An admin is someone entitled to see all project dashboards, statistics, and user information in order to run the project, assess performance, and track activity. An admin cannot override the constraints of the system to change the rights status of a volume.

Attribute: A rights code is composed of two parts. The first half is called the attribute, and it represents the copyright status of the work and facilitates access control. Examples of attributes used by CRMS are "ic," "icus," "pd," "pdus," and "und." There are twenty-six attributes (as of this writing), though most are not used in copyright determination. A list of attributes can be found at http://www.hathitrust.org/rights_database.

Candidates (pool): The candidates pool is a subset of volumes within HathiTrust whose metadata (date and place of publication, country of origin, current rights, etc.) indicate they are within scope for a defined CRMS copyright review project. The candidates pool will trend toward zero as work progresses; however, it may remain level or even increase as HathiTrust ingests new volumes that match the scope. Candidates are updated each night by a query run against the HathiTrust Rights Database. In some cases, volumes are dropped

GLOSSARY

from candidates due to a change in eligibility often stemming from a correction to their bibliographic metadata.

Catalog ID: The catalog ID is a unique identifier assigned by HathiTrust and Zephir that joins together related volume IDs of a particular work in the same edition. Each catalog ID in Zephir may have one or more than one volume ID associated with it, depending on how many copies of that work in that same edition are in HathiTrust. This relationship can be used to assign rights codes to duplicate volumes; however, a catalog ID may also represent volumes in a multipart monograph. In this case, the catalog ID does not indicate volumes that are exactly the same and should not be used for rights code inheritance without determination of individual parts.

Conflict: A conflict occurs when two reviews for a volume disagree on one or more critical pieces of information that would affect access to the work. For example, two independent reviews of the same work are in conflict where one reviewer selects "public domain" and the other selects "in copyright."

Enum/chron (enumeration and chronology): These are standard metadata used in library catalogs for serial publications and multipart monographs. The presence of enum/chron metadata in a record prevents inheritance of rights codes in CRMS because volumes that are part of a multipart monograph may be subject to different rights.

GLOSSARY

Expert reviewer: An expert reviewer is a reviewer who is specially trained to adjudicate conflicting reviews. Experts are selected from top performing reviewers to address conflicts generated by reviewers.

Exported determinations: Not all final determinations are sent to the HathiTrust Rights Database. Exported determinations are a subset of final determinations that meet criteria for export.

External admin: An external admin is a liaison from a partner institution that may not have authorization to perform copyright determinations but requires access to performance statistics of reviewers from their institution in order to make supervisory decisions.

Final determination: A final determination is the collective result of all reviews done on a volume (including, if necessary, an expert's adjudication). It is the result when that process is complete.

Inheritance: This takes place when a CRMS determination is exported to the Rights Database.

Inheriting volume(s): Inheriting volumes are all duplicate copies of a work (in that particular edition) in HathiTrust. After a source volume's rights code is exported to the HathiTrust Rights Database, volumes eligible for inheritance are automatically given the same rights code.

GLOSSARY

Inserts: Component parts in a larger work that were written or created by other authors and may be subject to different copyright terms. Illustrations, articles, quotations, lyrics, and diagrams are examples of "component parts" that could turn out to be inserts. An insert could be an extensive part of a larger work, but even a brief insert can be significant. The presence of an insert is one of the more common reasons why a CRMS reviewer may decide a volume should be set aside as "undetermined."

Multipart monograph: A work composed of more than one part in which the parts have been published over a span of time (usually several years). A multipart monograph can be a special problem in copyright determination because the parts of the work may be subject to different copyright laws—for example, a US work in which the first part was published in 1920, the second part in 1925, and the third in 1930. As a result, the individual parts have to be reviewed independently, even though technically they belong to the same work.

PageTurner: A HathiTrust application that enables authorized reviewers to view scanned page images. CRMS embeds a version of PageTurner in its interface, but it is a separate application owned and maintained by HathiTrust. HathiTrust access and authentication modules confirm when a user should have authorization to have access to it. If a request for access does not come from an approved IP address, PageTurner will restrict access to works in the public

GLOSSARY

domain. For more details about the application, see http://www.hathitrust.org/access_determination.

Priority: Priority codes route a volume through the CRMS system so it will be displayed to the appropriate user and in some cases restricted from view to other users. The majority of volumes are given Priority 0, which enables any reviewer to see them. Some volumes receive higher priority to ensure they will be reviewed more quickly and/or by a more experienced reviewer.

Reason: A rights code is composed of two parts. The second half is called the "reason," and it accounts for why the volume was given that copyright status. There are eighteen "reasons" (as of this writing) accounting for a number of different situations. A list of reasons can be found at http://www.hathitrust.org/rights_database.

Review: A review is an individual reviewer's judgment about the copyright status of a work. The reason for that judgment is stored in the system with a corresponding rights code. Depending on how a volume moves through the CRMS process, two or three reviews may accrue before a final determination is reached.

Reviewer/advanced reviewer: A reviewer is a person authorized to perform copyright determinations. A reviewer is moved up to the status of an advanced reviewer after demonstrating consistent and reliable understanding of the process. Advanced status requires less oversight of a reviewer's work.

GLOSSARY

Rights code: A shorthand term representing both the attribute and reason code of a determination.

Rights database: The repository of rights information for each digitized volume in HathiTrust. The Rights Database should not be confused with the CRMS database, which is a separate repository that includes more detailed metadata necessary for rights research. For further details, see https://www.hathitrust.org/rights_database.

Source volume: A source volume is the specific scan that has undergone manual review. A volume ID represents the source volume. Once one copy is reviewed in CRMS and becomes a source volume, then all the other copies associated with that particular catalog ID in Zephir may become "inheriting volumes," provided there is no indication of enum/chron in the catalog ID.

Status: Status codes indicate how far a volume has progressed through the review process and, to some degree, which path that volume is taking through the system (e.g., Did both reviewers agree or disagree?).

Super admin: A super admin has the highest level of permissions and may override system logic in order to review any volume, not constrained by the scope of any given candidate pool. Formal legal training is a consideration in granting this role. The system developer also has this role.

GLOSSARY

Swiss option: The Swiss option is an alternative to invalidation, which an expert reviewer may employ during adjudication to grant a neutral mark to a nonconforming review. Without this option, any reviews that do not match the expert's would count as errors in the reviewer's personal statistics. A Swiss option neutralizes the issue and avoids invalidating either reviewer. It is primarily useful in situations where there is complexity or a judgment call beyond the bounds of routine work.

Validation/invalidation rate: A validation rate is the percentage of an individual's reviews that either matched other reviewers' judgments or are deemed correct by experts. The statistic is represented as validation in the personal display. For the management team, it displays in the converse as invalidation. The validation rate is a broad measurement to test how closely a reviewer is aligned with the CRMS review process. Adjudications where an expert elects to apply the Swiss option do not count against a reviewer's validation rate. Instead, they are counted separately, influencing neither validation nor invalidation.

Volume: A volume in HathiTrust is not a "book" in the normal sense of that word but a unit of measurement indicating the unique scan representing one physical item. In line with common library binding practice, it may represent a discrete monograph, a single volume from a monographic series, or several items bound together. Scans of the same work but from different physical copies are treated as

GLOSSARY

unique volumes, and each one receives its own volume ID. Copyright determinations are made at the volume level.

Volume ID: The volume ID is an alphanumeric identifier assigned by HathiTrust and Zephir to a volume (e.g., mdp.39015005731453). Each scan representing a different physical copy of a work is assigned a unique volume ID.

Zephir: A bibliographic metadata management system the California Digital Library developed specifically for HathiTrust. Prior to Zephir's launch in fall 2013, HathiTrust had relied on Mirlyn, the University of Michigan's online catalog.

Resources

Cohen, Julie E., Lydia Loren, Ruth L. Okediji, and Maureen Anne O'Rourke, eds. *Copyright in a Global Information Economy*, 4th ed. (New York: Wolters Kluwer, 2015).

Cornell University. "Checklist for Conducting a Fair Use Analysis before Using Copyrighted Materials" (Revised for use by Cornell University from the "Checklist for Fair Use," a project of the IUPUI Copyright Management Center, directed by Kenneth D. Crews, Associate Dean of the Faculties for Copyright Management), accessed January 20, 2016, https://copyright.cornell.edu/policies/docs/Fair_Use_Checklist.pdf.

Crews, Kenneth D. *Copyright Law for Librarians and Educators: Creative Strategies and Practical Solutions*, 3rd ed. (Chicago: ALA Editions, 2012).

Europeana. "Public Domain Calculator," accessed January 20, 2016, http://archive.outofcopyright.eu/index.html.

Fishman, Stephen. *Copyright and the Public Domain* (New York: Law Journal Press, 2008).

Geller, Paul Edward, and Melville B. Nimmer. *International Copyright Law and Practice* (Newark, NJ: Matthew Bender, 2009).

Georgetown Law. "Copyright Law Research Guide," last modified December 8, 2015, http://www.law.georgetown.edu/library/research/guides/copyright.cfm.

Goldstein, Paul. *International Copyright: Principles, Law, and Practice*, 3rd ed. (Oxford: Oxford University Press, 2013).

RESOURCES

Hirtle, Peter. "Copyright Term and the Public Domain in the United States," last modified January 3, 2016, http://copyright.cornell.edu/resources/publicdomain.cfm.

Hirtle, Peter B., Emily Hudson, and Andrew T. Kenyon. *Copyright and Cultural Institutions: Guidelines for Digitization for US Libraries, Archives, and Museums* (Ithaca, NY: Cornell University Library, 2009).

Mannapperuma, Menesha A., Brianna L. Schofield, Andrea K. Yankovsky, Lila Bailey, and Jennifer M. Urban. "Is It in the Public Domain?," last modified May 27, 2014, https://www.law.berkeley.edu/files/FINAL_PublicDomain_Handbook_FINAL%281%29.pdf.

Nimmer, Melville B., and David Nimmer. *Nimmer on Copyright* (New York: Matthew Bender, 1978–).

Ockerbloom, John. "The Online Books Page: Copyright Registration and Renewal Records," accessed January 20, 2016, http://onlinebooks.library.upenn.edu/cce/.

Padfield, Tim. *Copyright for Archivists and Records Managers,* 5th ed. (London: Facet Publishing, 2015).

Patry, William. *Patry on Copyright* (Eagen, MN: Thomson/West, 2006).

Smith, Kevin L. *Owning and Using Scholarship: An IP Handbook for Teachers and Researchers* (Chicago: American Library Association, Association of College and Research Libraries, 2014).

Stanford University Libraries. "Copyright and Fair Use," accessed January 20, 2016, http://fairuse.stanford.edu.

RESOURCES

Stanford University Libraries & Academic Information Resources. "Copyright Renewal Database," accessed January 20, 2016, http://collections.stanford.edu/copyrightrenewals/.

Stim, Richard. *Getting Permission: How to License & Clear Copyrighted Materials Online & Off*, 5th ed. (Berkeley, CA: Nolo, 2013).

Sunstein Kann Murphy & Timbers. "Copyright Flowchart," accessed January 20, 2016, http://sunsteinlaw.com/practices/copyright-portfolio-development/copyright-pointers/copyright-flowchart/.

US Copyright Office. "Circulars and Brochures," accessed January 20, 2016, http://copyright.gov/circs/.

US Copyright Office. *Compendium of US Copyright Office Practices*, last modified December 22, 2014, http://copyright.gov/comp3/.

World Intellectual Property Organization. "WIPO Lex," accessed January 20, 2016, http://www.wipo.int/wipolex/en/.

- GETTING STARTED
- AT A GLANCE—OVERVIEW
- INVOLVING YOUR LEADERSHIP
- PROJECT SCOPING
- LEGAL
- PERSONNEL
- VERIFICATION
- FUNDING
- TECHNICAL
- PILOT PROJECTS

Index

access, 235–36
   authorizing reviewers for, 99–100
   categories of, 35
   to reviewed volumes, 13
access controls, 153–56
access modules, 177–78
active volumes, 131
administrators, 25–26, 39–40, 112, 122, 135, 156
Adobe Acrobat Professional, 106
AdobeConnect, 109
advanced elements, 153
advanced reviewers, 134–35, 155
   See also reviewers
advisory groups, 40–42, 53, 90–91, 104
Ahronheim, Judith, xvi
algorithms, 145–46, 156–57, 176, 182, 191
anonymous authors, 34
anthologies, 240
approximate death dates, 239
archival collections, 79–80, 82
Argentina, 205
attributes (rights code), 140
Australia, 73–74
author-based determinations, 23, 48–50, 194, 199–200
author death dates, 14, 48–50, 194, 205–6, 213, 215–19
   approximate, 239
   not found, 238

authority records, 214–20
authorization, 99–100, 154
authors
   additional, 83–84
   anonymous, 34
   names missing from title pages, 239
automated data e-mail, 109

backup data, 18
Barrie, J. M., 71–72
benchmarking, 110–11
Benson Latin American Collection, 201–8
Berne Convention for the Protection of Literary and Artistic Works, 62
Bibliographic API. *See under* HathiTrust
BlueJeans videoconferencing, 106
"bound-with" volumes, 226–27
browsers, 142

California Digital Library, 130
Camtasia Studio, 106–7
Canada, 67, 73–74
candidate pools, 45, 128, 172–74, 195–96, 203, 210, 222
candidates
   import, 173
   inheritance, 160, 188

INDEX

case law, 54
catalog ID, 130
cataloging practices, 219
Catalog of Copyright Entries (CCE), 14, 37, 59, 64, 76
Chesterton, G. K., 68–69
Circular 38b (US Copyright Office), 61–63
Class A works, 22, 44
Clement, Gail, 80–81
codes field, 34
collaborations, 31–32, 91–92, 95
communication, 39, 108–13
Compendium of US Copyright Office Practices (US Copyright Office), 64–65
compilations, 240
complex projects, 36–37, 74, 194
component parts, 133
computational resources, 18
conference calls, 109
conflicts, 135, 138, 157–58, 181–83
conflicts interface, 126
conflicts table, *185*
copyright
    as design problem, xv–xvii
    duration of, 26–27, 56–60, 67
    experts, 6–7, 54–55, 90–91
    formalities, 57–60
    international, 66–74
    notice, 50–51, 60

renewal, 33, 50, 56
review, 32–33
social bargain of, xv–xvi
specialists, 197
Copyright and Cultural Institutions (Hirtle, Hudson, and Kenyon), 80–81
Copyright and Publication Status of Pre-1978 Dissertations (Clement and Levine), 80–81
copyright law
    Argentina, 205
    Australia, 73–74
    Canada, 67, 73–74
    Germany, 69
    Spain, 68–69
    United Kingdom, 27–28, 70–74
    United States, 26–27, 56–60
Copyright Notice (US Copyright Office), 60–61
Copyright Office, US. *See* US Copyright Office
Copyright Restoration under the URAA (US Copyright Office), 62–62
Copyright Review Management System, US (CRMS-US), 54–55
    advisory working group, 42, 53
    background of, 125–27
    candidates for, 170–71
    code, 143
    database, 143–44
    decision tree, *229*

INDEX

exports, 190–91
review process, 168–78
rights/reason codes, 234
scope of, 43–45
toolkit, 1–4
wiki, *237*
Copyright Review Management System, World (CRMS-World), 66–74
candidates for, 171–72
decision tree, *230*
development of, 126–27
rights/reason codes, 235
scope of, 46–47
wiki, 236–37
Copyright Risk Management (Smith), 89
Copyright Term and the Public Domain in the United States (Hirtle), 29, 56–57
core elements, 142–52
core staff, 30
cost-share commitments, 19, 113, 121–22, *231*
country of origin, 170
critical thinking, 96
"CRMS South America" (Ovalle, Garstka, and Harper), 201
CRMS-US. *See* Copyright Review Management System, US
CRMS-World. *See* Copyright Review Management System, World
Crown Copyright, 73–74

dashboards, 165–66
databases, 66, 140, 143–44
data collection, 14–15, 205
date ranges, 146
deans, 39–40
death dates. *See* author death dates
decision points, 20–23
decision trees, 118, 180, *198*, 224–26, *225*, *229*, *230*
desired outcomes, 12, 196, 204, 211, 223
determinations, 139
author-based, 23, 48–49, 194, 199–200
exported, 139, 152
exporting to Rights Database, 190–91
final, 139
linking reviews with, 159
mismatches in, 111
number of, 96
Public Domain (PD) US, 235
Public Domain (PD) Worldwide, 236
range of, 17
undetermined/need further investigation (und/nfi), 16, 86–89, 139, 236
determinations table, 187
Deutsches Historisches Museum, 213
developers, 8–9, 18
Digital Public Library of America (DPLA), 18
dissertations, 21, 80–83

297

INDEX

"Dissertations, Theses, and Student Papers" (Hirtle, Hudson, and Kenyon), 80–81
distance learning, 103–4
distributed work, 92
Diversey v. Schmidly, 82
D-Lib Magazine, 212
documentation, 34
double reviews, 17, 36, 92, 115–18, 197–98
DPLA. *See* Digital Public Library of America
Durantaye, Katharina de la, 210
Durationator, 120
duration of copyright, 26–27, 56–60, 67

Electronic Resource Access Unit, 125–26
e-mail groups, 109
employee time, 25, 39
enumeration and chronology (enum/chron), 134
environmental distractions, 97
errors, 35–36, 92, 119
Estate of Martin Luther King, Jr., Inc. v. CBS, Inc., 79
Europeana, 18, 66
European Community, 69
expert adjudications, 184–86
expert reviewers, 36, 92, 111–12, 135, 155–58, 189, *233*
exported determinations, 139, 152

export inheritance, 187–88
external administrators, 112, 135, 155
    See also administrators
external checks, 19

filtering methods, 45
final determinations, 139
financial commitment, 25, 39, 121
flexibility, 122–23
flowcharting software, 107
foreign languages, 21, 118, 193–200, 206, 212, 239–40
formalities, 57–60
funding, 19–20, 25, 36–37, 121–24, 196, 204, 211, 217, 223

Garstka, Caron, 201
Geller, Paul Edward, 29, 66–68,
general counsel, 7, 16, 25–26, 40–41
general publications, 79
Germany, 69, 208–14
goals, 12, 196, 204, 211, 223
Goldstein, Paul, 68
good faith, 53–54
government works, 23
    See also state government documents (US)
graduate students, 206

298

INDEX

grants, 19
group IDs, 186
group training, 101–2
Gutmann, Bessie Pease, 87–88

Harper, Georgia, 201
HathiTrust, 18, 99–100
    Bibliographic API, 144
    database, 125–27, 152, 169, 190–91
    leadership, 41–42
    multiple entries in, 213
headset microphones, 106
HeinOnline, 55
heuristics, 145–46
Hirtle, Peter, 29, 56–57, 80–81
historical reviews, 110, 163–64, 173, 187
hold mechanisms, 159–60
Hudson, Emily, 80–81
Hugenholtz, Bernt, 68
Humboldt University of Berlin, 208–14

IC US/PD Worldwide, 236
illustrations, 76–77
ILMS grants, 126–27
ILSA research group, 195
IMLS. *See* Institute of Museum and Library Services

inactivity, 109, 113
Indiana University, 126
information gaps, 200
inheritance, 132–34, 160–61, 187–89
inheritance IDs, *133*
in-house verification, 115
in-scope works, 145–46, 170
inserts, 21, 75–78, 88–89, 117–18, 133
Institute of Museum and Library Services (IMLS), 18, 113
institutional funding, 124
interfaces, 9, 18, 125–27, 136–38, 148–51, 180, 199
international copyright, 66–74
International Copyright (Goldstein and Hugenholtz), 68
International Copyright Law and Practice (Geller and Nimmer), 29, 66–68,
Is It in the Public Domain? (Samuelson Law, Technology and Public Policy Clinic), 57, 60

JavaScript, 143
job descriptions, 112

Karle-Zenith, Anne, xvi
Kenyon, Andrew, 80–81

299

INDEX

King, Martin Luther, Jr., 79
King James Bible, 70–71

language experts, 31, 199
large-scale projects, 6, 18, 32–33, 91, 104
last in, first out (LIFO), 174n73
late authors, 239
    See also author death dates
Latin American works, 201–8
LC NAF. *See* Library of Congress Name Authority File
leadership, 25–26, 39–42
LEETHI. *See* Literaturas Españolas y Europeas del Texto al Hipermedia
legal issues, 15–16, 29–30, 53–93, 117–18
    case law, 54
    counsel, 91
    experts, 6–7
    general counsel, 7, 16, 25–26, 40–41
    resources, 54–55
    17 U.S.C. § 104A, 15, 61–64
    17 U.S.C. § 105, 64–65
Levine, Melissa, 18, 80–81, 210
LexisNexis, 55
liability, institutional, 39
Library of Congress Authorities, 151
Library of Congress Name Authority File (LC NAF), 218

LIFO. *See* last in, first out
Limited Times, LLC, 120
Literaturas Españolas y Europeas del Texto al Hipermedia (LEETHI), 195
locking mechanisms, 147, 175
Love's Blossom (Gutmann), 87–88

MARC, 146
matches, 181–83
matching funds, 121
MediaGallery, 107
MediaWiki, 106
metadata, 128–29, 144–46, 174–75, 212
Mirlyn, 130
missing pages, 181
"Mnemosine: The Digital Library of Rare and Forgotten Spanish Texts (1868–1939)" (research project), 195
monographs, multipart, 85–86, 133–34
multiple editions, 22
musical compositions, 241
MySQL, 141, 144

Name Authority Cooperative Program (NACO), 193, 214–20
name-based approach, 211
national treatment, 68–69

INDEX

native applications, 142
New General Catalog of Old Books and Authors (NGCOBA), 14
Nimmer, David, 29
Nimmer, Melville B., 29, 66–67
Nimmer on Copyright (Nimmer and Nimmer), 29, 54–55
non-divesting limited publications, 79
notes field, 34
notice and takedown procedures, 16, 89–90

Online Computer Library Center (OCLC) Connexion, 218
online resources, 54–55, 66, 151
    testing modules, 102
    training, 10, 103–4
Oracle, 144
orphan works, 78
output decisions, 35
Ovalle, Carlos, 201
overnight processing, 172–73, 175, 186–87

PageTurner, 136, 177–78
partitions, 196–99
partnerships, 91–92
pattern recognition, 96
performance thresholds, 17

periodicals, 22
Perl, 143–44
permissions, 93
personal stats display, 110
personnel, 30–32, 95–114
    See also reviewers; staffing
Peter Pan, 71–72
Phil Collins case, 69
photographs, 75–76
pilot projects, 193–228
Post Mortem Auctoris (PMA), 216
    See also author death dates
predicted public domain dates, 207
preplanning, 5–11
preproject verification, 116–17
priority, 136, 167
procedures, 118
process verification, 117–18
production numbers, 96
production readiness, 107
"progress toward goal" bar, 108
project management, 5–6, 16
projects
    building, 12–20
    design, 195–96, 203–4, 210–11, 216–17, 222–23
    preplanning, 5–11
    preproject verification, 116–17
    scope of, 12–13, 26–27, 43–52, 70

INDEX

provisional matches, 167, 183, *185*
public domain, xv–xvii
    predicted dates, 207
    variation between countries, 35
published/unpublished divide, 78
Puccini, 69
Python, 143

quality control, 9–10, 19, 36
Qualtrics, 105–6
queues, 141, 147–48, 174–77, 199

Rails, 143
Ray, Joyce, 210
reason (rights code), 140
records, wrong, 181
remote collaboration, 95
renewal of copyright, 33, 50, 56
re-review, 163, 186
    of candidate pool, 119
research tools, 58–60
resource commitment, 26, 39
restoration, 61–64
results verification, 119–20
reviewers, 10–11, 30–31, 154–55
    adding new, 17
    advanced, 134–35, 155

authorizing for access, 99–100
communication with, 108–10
equipment for, 97
expert, 36, 92, 111–12, 135, 155–58, 189, *233*
graduates students as, 206
job description, *232–33*
management, 9–10, 110–11
overseeing new, 167
performance tracking, 165
selecting, 95–96
See also personnel; staffing
review interface, 118, 141, 148–51
review process, 33, 138, 163, 168–91
review table, 141
rights codes, 140, 234–35
rights database, 140
risk tolerance, 39, 92
Ruby, 143

Samuelson Law, Technology and Public Policy Clinic, 57
sandbox, 17, 104–5, 168
scans, digital, 32, 99–100, 125, 206
scope of projects, 12–13, 26–27, 43–52, 70
Screencast.com, 107
Seadle, Michael, 210
search features, 163

INDEX

security, 19, 99–100, 144, 153–54
sheet music, 241
simultaneous publication, 63
single authorship, 238
Skype videoconferencing, 106
Smith, Kevin, 82, 89
social bargain of copyright, xv–xvi
source volumes, 131–32
Spain, 68–69, 193–200
staffing, 31, 122–23, 196, 204, 210, 217, 223
  See also personnel; reviewers
standardized education plans, 102
Stanford Copyright and Fair Use Center, 54–55
Stanford Copyright Renewal Database, xvii, 14, 22, 33, 44, 51, 58, 75, 127
start-up costs, 121
state government documents (US), 51–52, 221–28
"Statement for Access to In-Copyright Works in HathiTrust" (CRMS), 179
statistics reports, 165
status codes, 136–37, 182
subproject mechanism, 161–62
super administrators, 135, 155
  See also administrators
supervisors, 112–13
Swiss option, 138

takedown procedures, 89–90
team building, 5–11
technical considerations, 18–19, 31, 141–42
Template Toolkit, 143
territoriality, 67–68
"Testing the HathiTrust Copyright Search Protocol in Germany" (*D-Lib Magazine*), 212
Teubner-Verlag, 213
theses, 21, 80–83
third-party authored materials. *See* inserts
third-party examinations, 36, 115, 119
time commitments, 26, 97–99, 112–13
time frame of projects, 196, 203, 210, 217, 222
title pages, author names missing from, 239
training, 9–10, 17, 101–3, 104–7
translations, 21, 84–85
tutoring, 101–2

UMI. *See* University Microfilms International
undetermined/need further investigation (und/nfi) determinations, 16, 86–89, 139, 236
uniformity, 34
United Kingdom, 27–28, 70–74
United Nations, 93
United States, 26–27, 51–52, 56–60
  See also state government documents (US)

303

INDEX

Universidad Complutense de Madrid, 193–94
University Microfilms International (UMI), 81
University of California, Berkeley, 81
University of Michigan, 103, 125, 130, 143–44, 138
University of Minnesota, 126
University of New Mexico, 82
University of Texas at Austin, 201–8
University of Wisconsin, 126
unprocessed reviews, 163
unpublished works, 78–79
Uruguay Round Agreements Act (URAA), 15, 61–64
17 U.S.C. § 104A, 15, 61–64
17 U.S.C. § 105, 64–65
US Copyright Acts, 29, 54–55
    Section 101, 65
US Copyright Office, 22, 29, 55, 64–65, 120
    Catalog, 59
    Circular 38b, 62–63
user roles, 134–35
user types, 154–55

validation/invalidation rate, 137–38, 165
verification, 20, 35–36, 115–20

VG Wort, 213
video tutorials, 102
Virtual International Authority File (VIAF), xvii, 14, 33, 45, 63, 125, 151, 199, 209, 216
volume ID, 129
volunteers, 217

War Office seal, *73*
web-based applications, 143–44
Westlaw, 55
Wikipedia, 151, 199
Wilkin, John, xvi
WIPO Lex, 30, 66
workflow, 196–97, 205–6, 211–12, 217–19, 224
WorldCat, 63
World International Property Organization (WIPO), 30
World Trade Organization (WTO), 62
wrong records, 181

Zephir, 129–32, 169
Zoho chat, 108

CPSIA information can be obtained
at www.ICGtesting.com
Printed in the USA
BVOW07s0308040616
450704BV00003B/8/P